AQA

Religious Studies B

Religion and Morality

Marianne Fleming

Anne Jordan

Peter Smith

David Worden

Series editor

Cynthia Bartlett

OXFORD

UNIVERSITY PRESS

OXFORD
UNIVERSITY PRESS

Great Clarendon Street, Oxford, OX2 6DP, United Kingdom

Oxford University Press is a department of the University of Oxford.
It furthers the University's objective of excellence in research, scholarship,
and education by publishing worldwide. Oxford is a registered trade mark of
Oxford University Press in the UK and in certain other countries

Text © Marianne Fleming, Anne Jordan, Peter Smith and David Worden 2014
Original illustrations © Oxford University Press 2014

The moral rights of the authors have been asserted.

First published by Nelson Thornes Ltd in 2009
This edition published by Oxford University Press in 2014

British Library Cataloguing in Publication Data
Data available

978-1-4085-0514-4

10 9 8 7

Printed in China

Acknowledgements

Cover photograph/illustration: Alamy / Richard Levine
Illustrations: Rupert Besley, Paul McCaffrey (c/o Sylvie Poggio
Artists Agency) and Hart McLeod
Page make-up: Hart McLeod, Cambridge

Photo acknowledgements

Alamy: SAV / 5.6B; **Central Office of Information:** 3.11A;
Corbis: Dominique Derda / France 2/ 6.9C; Narong Sangnak/epa
/ 6.9A; **Dignitas:** 2.8Aa; **Disaster Emergency Committee:**
6.8C; **Fairtrade:** 6.7A; **Fotolia:** 1.3A; 1.10Aa; 1.10Ab; 1.10Ac;
2.2B; 2.7A; 3C; 3.1A; 3.1B; 3.1C; 3.2A; 3.3A; 3.4A; 3.4B; 3.5A;
3.6A; 3.6C; 4.3B; 4.6A; 4.7A; 4.7B; 4.8A; 4.8B; 4.9A; 4.9B; 4.9C;
4.10A; 5C; 5.1A; 5.1B; 6.1A; 6.5B; 6.7B; **Getty Images:** AFP /
2.10B; Time & Life Pictures / 1.6A; **iStockphoto:** 1.8A; 1.9A;
1.9B; 1.12A; 2C; 2.1B; 2.3A; 2.3B; 2.6A; 2.6B; 2.9B; 2.11A; 3.2B;
3.6B; 3.7B; 3.8B; 3.9A; 4C; 4.1A; 4.1B; 4.2A; 4.2B; 4.3A; 4.4A;
4.5B; 4.6B; 4.10B; 4.11A; 5.2A; 5.4A; 5.5A; 5.7B; 5.11A; 6C;
6.2B; 6.2C; 6.3A; 6.4A; 6.5A; 6.6A; 6.7C; 6.10A; **Islamic Relief
Worldwide:** 6.6B; **Mirrorpix:** 2.2A; 2.9A; 5.10B; **Newsquest
(North East) Ltd:** 5.10C; **NGDT:** 1.5B; **NHS Blood and
Transplant:** 1.6B; 1.6C; **PA Photos:** 5.3A; Jessica Gow/Scanpix
/ 3.10A; **Peter Smith:** 2.1A; 5.8A; 5.9A; **Rex Features:** 5.3B;
GTV Archive / 1.2B; Israel Image / 5.7A; Julian Hamilton / 2.8Ab;
Ray Tang; 5.6A; Stuart Atkins / 1.3B; Photonews Service Ltd /
4.5A; **Reuters:** STR / 6.8B; 6.9B; **The Daily Telegraph 2008:**
Christopher Jones / 1.5A; **Topfoto:** UPPA / 4.4B.

Text acknowledgements

Scripture quotations taken from the Holy Bible, New
International Version. Copyright © 1978, 1984 by International
Bible Society. Used by permission of Hodder & Stoughton, a
division of Hodder Headline Ltd. All rights reserved. "NIV"
is a registered trademark of International Bible Society. UK
trademark number 1448790.

1.1: Definition of 'Religion' from CONCISE OXFORD ENGLISH
DICTIONARY edited by Soanes & Stevenson, Oxford University
Press, 2008. Reprinted with permission of Oxford University
Press. 1.5: Bigger than a man landing on the moon', by
Judith Woods, Daily Telegraph, 21st July 2008, reprinted with

permission of Telegraph Media Group Limited. 'I feel as if I've
spent half my life waiting', by Judith Woods, Daily Telegraph,
22nd July 2008, reprinted with permission of Telegraph Media
Group Limited. 1.6: Monstrous attack on human rights', by
Jonathan Petre, Daily Telegraph, 24th March 2008, reprinted
with permission of Telegraph Media Group Limited. 1.8: Short
quote by The Archbishop Rowan Williams. Reprinted with
kind permission. 2.1: Short quote by Professor Allan Kellehear.
Reprinted with kind permission of the author. 2.5, 3.5, 3.7, 4.1,
4.5, 4.8, 5.7 & 6.6: Extracts from THE HOLY QURAN TRANSLATION
AND COMMENTARY by Abdullah Yusuf Ali. Reprinted with
permission of IPCI - Islamic Vision, 434 Coventry Road, Small
Heath, Birmingham B10 0UG UK. 2.7: Short extract reprinted
with the kind permission of the General Medical Council.
3.4 'Cannabis should be reclassified, Brown says', by Robert
Winnett, Daily Telegraph, 22nd April 2008, reprinted with
permission of Telegraph Media Group Limited. 3.9: Darren's
Story reprinted with permission of www.drugsline.org. 4.2:
Headline 'Two teenage boys stabbed... It's just another day
of gang warfare in Peckham' by Benedict Moore-Bridger,
Evening Standard, 14/5/08 pg 6. Reprinted with permission of
Solo Syndication. 5.1: 'Sri Isopanisad Text courtesy of The
Bhaktivedanta Book Trust International, Inc www.krishna.com.
Used with permission. 5.10: Short extract from 'Rags to riches
to rags again for £10m lotto man' by Chris Brooke, Daily Mail,
11/2/08 pg 9. Reprinted with permission of Solo Syndications.
5.10 'Muslims shun project funded by lottery' by Ruth Gled
Hill, The Times, 28th April 2007, reprinted with permission of
NI Syndication Ltd. 6.8: Quote by Mahatma Gandhi. Reprinted
with kind permission of Navajivan Trust.

Although we have made every effort to trace and contact all
copyright holders before publication this has not been possible
in all cases. If notified, the publisher will rectify any errors or
omissions at the earliest opportunity.

Contents

Nelson Thornes has worked to make sure that this book offers you the best possible support for your GCSE course. You can be sure that it gives you just what you need when you are preparing for your exams.

■ How to use this book

This book covers everything you need for your course.

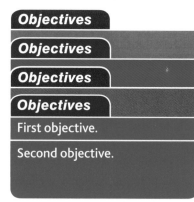

Learning Objectives

At the beginning of each section or topic you'll find a list of Learning Objectives based on the requirements of the specification, so you can make sure you are covering everything you need to know for the exam.

Study Tips

Don't forget to look at the Study tips throughout the book to help you with your study and prepare for your exam.

> **Study tip**
>
> Don't forget to look at the Study tips throughout the book to help you with your study and prepare for your exam.

Practice Questions

These offer opportunities to practise doing questions in the style that you can expect in your exam so that you can be fully prepared on the day.

AQA examination questions are reproduced by permission of the Assessment and Qualifications Alliance.

Introduction

This book is written specifically for GCSE students studying the AQA Religious Studies Specification B, *Unit 3:Religion and Morality*. Morality is all about deciding what is the right and wrong action in any situation. For a religious person, their faith will influence these decisions so you need to know and understand what religious people believe.

You do not have to be religious to study this course. You simply need to be interested in thinking about and discussing different religious and moral questions. You also need to be willing to think deeply about your own opinions on religious and moral questions, and be prepared to express them orally and in writing. You will be encouraged to become familiar with the arguments put forward by other people and to reflect on them so you can explain and evaluate your own reasoned opinions.

■ Topics in this unit

In the examination you will be asked to answer four questions, based on four of the following six topics.

Religious attitudes to matters of life

This topic examines beliefs and teachings about life, considering how advances in medical technology can affect people's lives and some of the decisions they may have to make.

Religious attitudes to the elderly and death

You will apply religious principles about the sanctity and value of life to matters affecting the elderly. You will also consider medical technology related to death and dying, and consider what may happen after death.

Religious attitudes to drug abuse

You will consider religious ideas about the body and mind, and how a person's life may be affected by using different types of drugs, including legal, social and illegal drugs.

Religious attitudes to crime and punishment

This topic looks at religious ideas about human nature, wrongdoing and the punishment of offenders. It considers different types of crime, reasons why people commit them, and the range and purpose of different punishments.

Religious attitudes to rich and poor in British society

You will be made aware of religious beliefs and teachings about wealth and poverty. You will consider why both rich and poor exist in Britain, as well as ways in which poverty can be overcome and who is responsible for helping the poor.

Religious attitudes to world poverty

This topic deals with religious beliefs and teachings about poverty in less-economically developed countries. You will consider different types of projects aimed at reducing poverty and evaluate the need for them together with their effectiveness.

■ Assessment guidance

The questions set in the examination will allow you to refer in your answers to the religion(s) you have studied. There will be six questions, each worth 18 marks, of which you must answer any four. To enable you to practise the type of question that will be set in the examination, each chapter has an assessment guidance section at the end. This will help you to write better answers. To assist you in this, you will be asked to mark a given example.

In questions targeted at what you know and understand (AO1), you receive most marks if you explain and develop your answer.

In evaluation questions (AO2), asking for your own ideas together with religious ones, use the mark scheme below. Make sure that you understand the differences between the standard of answer for each level, and what you need to do to achieve full marks.

Examination questions will test two assessment objectives:

AO1	Describe, explain and analyse, using knowledge and understanding.	50%
AO2	Use evidence and reasoned argument to express and evaluate personal responses, informed insights, and differing viewpoints.	50%

Levels of response mark scheme for six-mark evaluation questions

Levels	Criteria for AO1	Criteria for AO2	Quality of written communication	Marks
0	Nothing relevant or worthy of credit	An unsupported opinion or no relevant evaluation	The candidate's presentation, spelling punctuation and grammar seriously obstruct understanding	0 marks
Level 1	Something relevant or worthy of credit	An opinion supported by simple reason	The candidate presents some relevant information in a simple form. The text produced is usually legible. Spelling, punctuation and grammar allow meaning to be derived, although errors are sometimes obstructive	1 mark
Level 2	Elementary knowledge and understanding, e.g. two simple points	An opinion supported by one developed or two simple reasons		2 marks
Level 3	Sound knowledge and understanding	An opinion supported by one well developed reason or several simple reasons. **N.B. Candidates who make no religious comment should not achieve more than Level 3**	The candidate presents relevant information in a way which assists with the communication of meaning. the text produced is legible. Spelling, punctuation and grammar are sufficiently accurate not to obscure meaning	3 marks
Level 4	A clear knowledge and understanding with some development	An opinion supported by two developed reasons with reference to religion		4 marks
Level 5	A detailed answer with some analysis, as appropriate	Evidence of reasoned consideration of two different points of view, showing informed insights and knowledge and understanding of religion	The candidate presents relevant information coherently, employing structure and style to render meaning clear. The text produced is legible. Spelling, punctuation and grammar are sufficiently accurate to render meaning clear	5 marks
Level 6	A full and coherent answer showing good anaiysis, as appropriate	A well-argued response, with evidence of reasoned consideration of two different points of view showing informed insights and ability to apply knowledge and understanding of religion effectively		6 marks

Note: In evaluation answers to questions worth only 3 marks, the first three levels apply. Questions which are marked out of 3 marks do not ask for two views, but reasons for your own opinion.

Successful study of this unit will result in a Short Course GCSE award. Study of one further unit will provide a Full Course GCSE award. Other units in Specification B, which may be taken to achieve a Full Course GCSE award are:

Unit 1 Religion and Citizenship
Unit 2 Religion and Life Issues
Unit 4 Philosophy of Religion in Society
Unit 5 Religious Expression in Society
Unit 6 Worship and Key Beliefs.

1 Religious attitudes to matters of life

1.1 Religion and morality

■ Definitions

Deciding the meaning of the word 'religion' is quite difficult. The *Concise Oxford Dictionary* defines religion as:

> 66 *the belief in a superhuman controlling power, especially in a personal God or gods entitled to obedience and worship ... the expression of this in worship ... a particular system of faith and worship.* 99

Whilst this seems a good definition, it appears to leave out the world's fourth-biggest religion, Buddhism, which has no God or gods entitled to obedience and worship.

Discussion activity

With a partner, try to come up with a better definition of the word 'religion'. Be prepared to share it with the rest of the class.

Morality is slightly easier to define, although it is often confused with **ethics**, which is closely related. Morality refers to personal decisions about what is right and wrong behaviour, and following those decisions in everyday life. Ethics refers to the study of the theory of morality, which helps to inform these personal decisions.

■ Making moral decisions

We all make moral decisions every day. We often do this without giving it a second thought because it seems to come naturally to us. However, because humans are thinking beings, we tend to base these decisions on certain principles. For example, people may have the principle to 'do your best not to cause anyone to suffer' and therefore they would try not to act unkindly or violently towards others.

Activity

1 Spend a couple of minutes thinking carefully about the principles you base your moral decisions on. Write them down and then compare them with the principles your neighbour has written.

A

There are two common types of morality.

Absolute morality

Absolute morality is where a person has a principle such as 'do not cause anyone to suffer', and never changes from that. This may mean that they would not fight in a war because it involves causing suffering to others.

Relative morality

Relative morality is where a person has a principle, but will adapt it to certain situations. Therefore, if they have the same principle, 'do not cause anyone to suffer', they may decide to fight in a war because although it causes suffering, a war may prevent greater suffering in the future.

Activity

2   Using the example of 'always be compassionate to people', explain the difference between absolute and relative morality.

◼ So how does religion fit into this?

Believers have no difficulty fitting their religious beliefs into their morality. It may be more of a challenge for them to stick to their moral principles, however, because they believe that if they break their code of morality, they will be offending against their religion and going against God.

Some religions seem to make it easier than others. For an ultra-orthodox Jew, trying to obey 613 laws from the Torah, it may seem fairly simple. After all, obeying 613 laws does not seem to leave many decisions to make. It is, of course, not quite so simple, because many of the laws are open to interpretation.

Some other religions give general principles rather than laws. The Buddhist Eightfold Path gives guidance about what is right, and the Jewish and Christian advice to 'love your neighbour' (which in essence is in all religions) leaves a lot of room for interpretation. However, they form a good basis for a code of morality which is developed by adding detail based on further religious teaching. In that way, religion and morality are strongly linked for believers.

This book considers six moral issues and gives religious teachings that influence the moral choices that believers have to make about them.

Activities

3   Carefully explain the link between religion and morality.

4   'Basing morality on religious belief is a good idea.' What do you think? Explain your opinion.

Summary

You should now know and understand the meanings of 'religion' and 'morality' and be able to link them together in making decisions.

Key terms

Morality: a system of ethics about what is right or wrong.

Ethics: the theory relating to morality.

Absolute morality: what is morally right and wrong applies to all circumstances, at all times.

Relative morality: what is morally right or wrong in any situation depends upon its particular circumstances.

WHY CAN'T YOU MAKE IT EASIER, GOD?

B

Study tip

In this course, make sure you refer to the religious principles that guide the moral decisions raised by the topics you study.

1.2 Why is life special?

Am I special?

The simple answer to that question is certainly yes. Maybe you don't realise quite how special you are. Although the raw materials (various simple chemicals and several litres of water) that make up your body cost just a few pounds, you are worth much more than that. We are all made up of the same chemicals, but we are all unique.

In 1818, the novelist Mary Shelley published a novel about a 'human monster' created by Victor Frankenstein out of spare body parts. The hardest task Frankenstein faced was to make his creation live. A convenient thunder and lightning storm solved the problem and unleashed Frankenstein's creation onto the world of the living. Nearly 200 years later, fiction has still not become fact. Life can only be created from the living, not from the dead. That is one reason why many think life is so special.

The sanctity of life

For a religious person, the fact that life is special leads on to the concept of the **sanctity of life**. Apart from Buddhism, all the major religions believe God was responsible for creating the original life forms. Many believe that these have evolved naturally (or perhaps with God's help) over millions of years, leading to the situation we have today. Others believe that the creation story their religion teaches is literally correct. This is another reason why life is special – it was first created by God and he still takes responsibility for it. This means that no person has the right to damage or destroy life, an idea that clearly has an impact on many issues related to matters of life. Of course, it is not quite that easy, because nobody can prove when life actually begins. Therefore issues such as embryology and genetic engineering are more complicated than they may at first appear.

The value of life

The **value of life** is also an important consideration. Although for some people it is not necessarily a religious idea, for others it is. Some people might interpret the value of life just in financial terms – is the benefit of a life (human or animal) worth the money that is being spent on it or will a life be improved sufficiently to justify the cost? If the answer to either of these questions is no, then the life is perhaps of limited value and maybe should not exist or great efforts should not be made to keep it going. However, other people would say that you should not think in this way because life itself is more valuable than money. They may question whether one person's life can ever be more valuable than another's. So it is important to think about what we mean by value.

Objectives

Appreciate religious ideas about why life is special.

Begin to apply these ideas to matters of life.

Beliefs and teachings

Don't you know that you yourselves are God's temple and that God's Spirit lives in you?

1 Corinthians 3:16

I'm sure I got the ingredients right, but I don't think it'll ever turn into a human being, no matter how many times I stir it.'

A

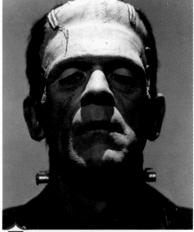

B *Life can only be created from the living, unlike Frankenstein's monster*

Activity

1 What do you think is meant by value in the context of the value of life? Compare your thoughts with those of a partner.

Discuss with a partner whether you think life that appears to have limited value should exist or not.

The quality of life

In assessing the value of life, many people, whether religious believers or not, consider whether a particular life will be comfortable and free from pain. Others develop this further by asking whether the person will be able to live with freedom, dignity and, for religious believers, the possibility of accessing or experiencing God – if so, this could be seen as a good **quality of life**. However, if their life is unlikely to be of sufficient quality, then perhaps they should be allowed to die. An example of this is a life-saving operation. Even if the operation will save a person's life, should it take place if the person is going to suffer extreme pain or disability for the rest of their life?

All three of the above ideas are relevant to matters of life and you will meet them throughout this topic.

Activities

2 **a** Copy the Venn diagram. Add ideas to explain the term in each circle.

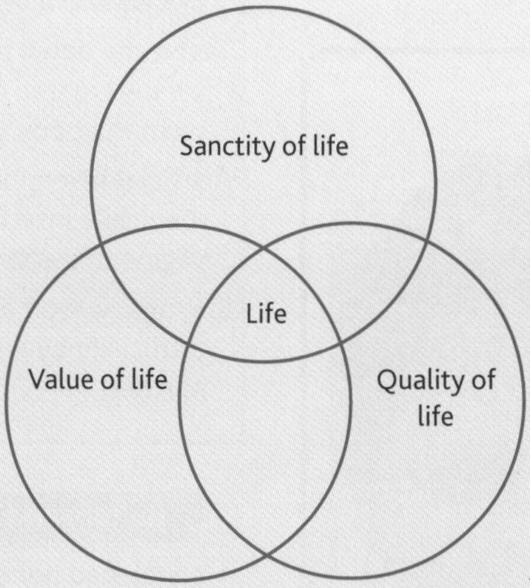

b Compare your diagram with a neighbour's and add anything you think is necessary. Try to persuade your neighbour to add one of your ideas.

3 How would you define a good quality of life? Give some examples to explain your answer.

Extension activities

1 Do you think a person's life should be saved regardless of the cost? Say why. What about an animal's life?

2 Are some people's lives worth more than other people's? Explain the reasons for your view.

Beliefs and teachings

God sends us and we take birth.

Adi Granth 1239

Study tip

You may be asked a specific question about these three ideas in your examination. Even if not, it is likely that you will be able to use some or all of them in other questions in this unit.

Key terms

Sanctity of life: life is sacred because it is God-given.

Value of life: the value of a person over and above physical value.

Quality of life: a measure of fulfilment.

Summary

You should now be able to discuss religious ideas about why life is special and apply them to matters of life.

The choice to have children

The choice of whether to have children or not is available to many people nowadays. Those who do not want children for any reason can enjoy a full sex life using contraception to prevent pregnancy. The morning-after pill or, later on, abortion can also be considered. On the other hand, thanks to **fertility treatment** provided by medical science and technology, many couples with fertility problems can still have children if they want them. Whereas in the past it was thought that God decided who should and should not have children, people are now much more able to make their own choices, even if they do need some help from science.

Discussion activities

1 Why do you think people want to have children?

2 Do you think people have a right to have children, even if they are infertile? Give your reasons.

In vitro fertilisation – IVF

Case study

Louise Brown

In November 1977, Lesley and John Brown, having been referred to Dr Patrick Steptoe a year previously because Lesley's fallopian tubes were blocked, agreed to undergo experimental **in vitro fertilisation (IVF)** treatment in the hope that she would conceive. Dr Steptoe took an egg from one of Lesley's ovaries and in a glass tube fertilised it with John's sperm. It was then placed in a special solution designed to nurture the egg as it began to divide. Two days later, he implanted the tiny embryo into Lesley's uterus and waited. On 25 July 1978, Lesley gave birth to a healthy girl they called Louise – the world's first '**test-tube baby**' conceived outside the mother's body in glass, the literal meaning of 'in vitro'.

A *Louise Brown – the world's first 'test-tube baby'*

Objectives

Gain knowledge and understanding of fertility treatment, especially in vitro fertilisation (IVF) and surrogacy.

Reflect on the need for fertility treatment and surrogacy.

Key terms

Fertility treatment: medical procedure to assist an infertile couple to have a child.

In vitro fertilisation (IVF): a scientific method of making a woman pregnant, which does not involve sex. Conception occurs via sperm and egg being placed into a test tube.

Test-tube baby: term used for a baby created outside of the woman's body.

Artificial insemination: sperm medically inserted into the vagina to assist pregnancy.

Surrogacy: woman's egg fertilised artificially by another woman's partner.

Beliefs and teachings

Hannah had none [children] … and the Lord had closed her womb.

1 Samuel 1:2, 5

B   *Many couples can now choose whether to have children or not*

Since 1977, in vitro fertilisation has become commonplace and helped couples who have no hope of having their own children to become parents. The procedure has hardly changed since that historic day although it is now common for more than one egg to be fertilised and more than one embryo to be implanted in the hope of a greater chance of success. Success rates are still quite low, however, and many couples have to undergo treatment several times before the embryo implants itself into the uterus wall, develops into a foetus and after 38 weeks is born as a baby. As you may imagine, not everybody was in favour of this procedure.

Beliefs and teachings

For you created my inmost being; you knit me together in my mother's womb ... my frame was not hidden from you when I was made in the secret place.

Psalm 139:13, 15

⬤⬤ links

The terms 'embryo' and 'human genetic engineering' are defined and covered in more detail on page 20.

Study tip

You need to practise arguing an opinion you disagree with.

⬤⬤ links

To read about artificial insemination in more detail and possible concerns about it, see page 14.

Activity

1 **a** Spend five minutes preparing an argument either for or against IVF.

b Spend a further two minutes thinking of questions to ask somebody who thinks differently from you.

c Be prepared to present your case and answer questions from others who disagree with you.

◼ Surrogacy

Fertility treatment can also be used to 'impregnate' a surrogate mother. It is usual for the surrogate mother's egg and sperm from the intended father to be used via **artificial insemination** treatment (traditional **surrogacy**). However, if the intended mother has working ovaries, their 'genetic' child can be conceived by using IVF to fertilise the mother's own eggs and implanting them into the surrogate mother's womb (gestational surrogacy). Once the baby is born, it is handed over to the couple for whom she carried it. Under British law, she can be paid expenses but not a fee.

After the child is born, the intended father will put his name on the birth certificate as the father of the child. This automatically gives him equal rights over the child with the surrogate mother. If he does not do this, he is advised to enter into a Parent Responsibility Agreement with the surrogate mother, which gives them equal rights over the child. After six weeks the couple can apply for a Parental Order. This gives them full parental rights over the child and the surrogate mother loses all the rights she had in the first six weeks.

Activity

2 Do you agree with surrogacy? Give your reasons.

Research activity 🔍

Find out more about surrogacy by looking at www.surrogacy.org.uk

Summary

You should now be able to discuss the need for, and use of, fertility treatment and surrogacy and the moral issues associated with them.

1.4   Artificial insemination

What is artificial insemination?

Artificial insemination has been used in farming for many years as a way of ensuring that selective breeding produces animals that are likely to produce the best meat or dairy products. Without its use, such products might be in short supply and more expensive. No one seems to mind farmers using this process with their livestock, but some people express concern about its use with humans.

Discussion activity

1. a   Discuss with a partner whether we should have different rules for medical treatment of humans and animals. Think of two reasons why we should and two reasons why we shouldn't.
   b   Share your ideas with the rest of the class. You could then write down the best three reasons for each opinion.

Human artificial insemination is where sperm is produced by masturbation, collected and inserted into the vagina of a woman in the hope that fertilisation will take place and she will become pregnant. There are two types of artificial insemination, depending on where the sperm comes from:

- **Artificial insemination by husband (AIH)** – this is where the sperm used comes from the husband or male partner of the woman hoping to become pregnant
- **Artificial insemination by donor (AID or DI)** – sperm is donated (for a small fee) by a male volunteer and, after being screened for diseases such as HIV, is used in the same way as in AIH. Children conceived in this way gain the legal right to know the identity of their genetic father if they want to when they reach the age of 18.

Should we use artificial insemination?

Both methods involve masturbation to produce the semen which contains the sperm. Some religions or denominations forbid this (e.g. Roman Catholicism and Judaism) because masturbation is seen as 'spilling the seed' that could produce life.

Whilst most people are in favour of AIH being used if it is the only way for a woman to have a child, many are against AID. This may be because:

- the donor is a stranger
- inserting the sperm from a man other than the woman's husband could be seen as adultery
- it allows an unmarried woman to have a child and bring it up on her own
- it allows a gay couple to have a child and bring it up in a 'single-sex home'

Objectives

Gain knowledge and understanding of different types of human artificial insemination.

Evaluate the moral issues associated with fertility treatment.

Study tip

If you are asked in an examination to explain reasons why some people think something, do not use bullet points because an explanation needs to have more detail and possibly examples.

Key terms

Artificial insemination by husband (AIH): when a woman is made pregnant by the sperm of her husband, but not through having sexual relations with him.

Artificial insemination by donor (AID or DI): when a woman is made pregnant by the sperm of a man other than her partner, but not through having sexual relations with him.

- the child might become very upset when they find out their genetic father (donor) is different from the father who brought them up
- the donor might be unhappy that his identity could be revealed to his genetic children.

Beliefs and teachings

By Divine Law are beings created.

Adi Granth

Activities

1. a Rank the six reasons (in italics above) why some people are against AID, with the most important reason first.

   b Compare your ranking with your partner's.

2. Think of some reasons why people might be in favour of AID (you could perhaps reverse some of the arguments against).

3. What is the main difference between artificial insemination and IVF?

Extension activity

Reflect on how you think someone would feel if at the age of 18 they found out their genetic father donated the sperm by which they were conceived. Do you think they would mind? Would they want to find out who the donor was? Would they want to meet him?

A *Do you think they'll have us?*

Whilst most people are generally in favour of fertility treatment whether it is artificial insemination or IVF, there are some who are not. The main reason for being opposed to fertility treatment is that it is not seen as natural, and is therefore against God, or that the 'wrong people' could become parents. On the other hand, on the grounds of compassion, the beliefs that everybody has the right to be a parent and that there is a very good chance that the child will be loved and brought up well lead many people to accept or welcome this relatively new technology. A religious believer may say that God has given people the intelligence to develop the technology to perform IVF, so it should be used. However, success rates are not high, although improving, and the process, especially IVF, is expensive, with no guarantee that pregnancy will result.

Summary

You should now be able to discuss the need for, and use of, artificial insemination and the moral issues associated with it.

1.5 Fertility treatment – a case study

■ 'Bigger than a man landing on the moon'

In the 30 years since Louise Brown became the world's first 'test-tube baby' in 1978, 111,633 children have been born in Britain because of IVF. Dr Patrick Steptoe, who pioneered the treatment with Professor Robert Edwards, described what they had achieved in assisting Louise Brown to be born as 'bigger than a man landing on the moon'.

Discussion activity

Do you think the birth of Louise Brown can be described as 'bigger than a man landing on the moon'? Discuss this with a partner and think of some reasons for your opinion.

Objectives

Gain deeper understanding of fertility treatment by looking at a real-life case study.

Evaluate issues related to the case study.

Case study

Gift of life for the Adlam family

Georgina Adlam's conception was no ordinary conception. Her parents, Sue and Andrew, had been trying unsuccessfully for a baby for some time but when Sue was 32, she had an early menopause. This left her unable to produce any eggs, thereby ruling out the possibility of her having a child through **sexual intercourse**.

Ten years later, after having considered adopting a child but rejecting the idea in favour of IVF using egg donation, Sue and Andrew committed themselves to expensive treatment by registering Sue as a private patient at a local clinic attached to a hospital. She had earlier been rejected for fertility treatment on the National Health Service because Andrew, her husband, had fathered a child in a previous marriage. A year later, an egg donor was found. She produced 17 eggs, of which 13 were fertilised with Andrew's sperm. Two of these fertilised eggs were implanted into Sue's womb and the remaining 11 were frozen for possible use in the future. Georgina was born as a result of this treatment and owes her life completely to IVF technology.

Five years after Georgina's birth, Sue described the relationship she has with her daughter:

'We love Georgina utterly and, because I carried her for nine months, she is completely mine – ours. She's the image of my husband but like me in character. The egg may have come from another woman, but she received nourishment from my body and was bathed in my hormones. I couldn't have loved my own biological child more. She knows that Mummy really wanted a baby but didn't have an egg, so a nice lady gave me one of hers.'

Sue and Andrew wanted to give Georgina a brother or sister but two attempts at implanting the remaining fertilised eggs that had been frozen were unsuccessful. As a result, they were left looking for another donor. However, in 2005 the legal right of donors to remain anonymous was reversed, which means they are now harder to recruit. Now it is more likely that donors are women who are undergoing fertility treatment themselves and who are willing to share their unwanted eggs provided the woman receiving them is prepared to pay the clinic bills for the donor's treatment as well as their own.

Key terms

Sexual intercourse: sexual activity involving more than one person, for reasons of procreation or pleasure.

A The Adlams, with their daughter, Georgina, who was conceived using IVF treatment

> ❝ *I feel as if I've spent half my life waiting, but, as anyone who's ever suffered from infertility knows, what keeps you going through all the sadness is the prospect of an amazing miracle.* ❞
>
> *Sue Adlam*

Research activity

Find out more about egg and sperm donation for use in IVF at www.ngdt.co.uk

■ Issues for the child

In addition to the cost of fertility treatment, the low chance of success in becoming pregnant and the removal of the legal right of donors to remain anonymous, there may also be implications for the child.

The parents must think carefully about whether and the best time to tell their child that their conception was as a result of IVF. Some children may react badly, feel they are in some way different, or be bullied at school if people find out. If their conception was by AID, the child may want to discover who their biological father is, which could cause upset and division in the family. However, given the difficulties their parents went through to ensure their conception, it is probable that they will feel wanted, loved and cared for, and able to overcome the potential problems.

B   *Give Hope, Give Life logo*

Activities

1   a   Reread the Adlams' story. Make a note of each moral issue (you should find at least five).

    b   For each moral issue, write down whether you think it is morally right or morally wrong.

    c   Choose one issue you have decided is morally right and one you think is morally wrong. Write a short paragraph for each, explaining your reasons.

2   Around 1 in 4 IVF treatments result in pregnancy. Do you think it is worth it in view of the cost (up to £10,000 per treatment)?

Study tip

You are not expected to use quotes in your examination, but if you do, try to use them accurately. They are a way of developing your ideas and gaining marks.

Summary

You should now be able to discuss the moral issues associated with fertility treatment in more depth and in relation to a real-life case study.

Extension activity

Do you think IVF is an 'amazing miracle'? Carefully explain why.

A major breakthrough in transplant surgery

Case study

The first heart transplant

On 3 December 1967, a new medical technique, which many people thought impossible, was tried out in Cape Town, South Africa. Dr Christiaan Barnard led a 30-person medical team and successfully transplanted a donor heart taken from the victim of a fatal motor accident into a patient suffering from heart disease. The patient, a man named Louis Washkansky, had volunteered himself for the new surgery. Although the operation was a success, Louis Washkansky died 18 days later from a lung infection, which was likely to have been caused by the treatment.

Transplant surgery is the replacement of a faulty organ with a healthy organ (e.g. heart or lung) taken from a donor, usually shortly after the donor's brain death. However, kidney and bone marrow donations, for example, are given by live donors. Organs are kept functioning by keeping the dead body on a ventilator until the patient is ready to receive them. Live donors primarily donate a single kidney or part of their liver, small bowel or pancreas. Transplant surgery was first performed in 1905 when a cornea (part of the eye) was successfully transplanted. The first kidney transplant was in 1954, but Dr Christiaan Barnard's heart transplant was a medical first. It is now performed regularly and successfully throughout the world, along with other transplants. The development of new and better drugs to prevent the body from rejecting the new organ has ensured that transplant surgery nowadays has a high success rate. However, the success rate is not 100% and some of the anti-rejection drugs can have serious side effects on some people. Organs for transplant cannot be sold in Britain.

Discussion activity

1. 'They are my organs which God gave me. Nobody is having them even when I am dead.' Discuss this quotation with a partner and be prepared to share your ideas with a larger group if asked to.

Donors have to give permission for their organs to be used – some carry an organ donor card or convey their wishes by registering on the organ donor register, to remove any doubt. Despite this, the next of kin still have to give permission for organs to be removed. People may wish to be a donor to 'help someone live after their death' out of compassion, because they can help to provide a good quality of life for someone else or because they believe in the sanctity and value of life.

It is now possible for organs from some animals (especially pigs) to be used for transplant. Some people happily accept this, although others think it is a step too far. Some Muslims would be prepared to accept a pig's organ as a last resort despite not being allowed to eat its meat.

Objectives

Understand basic information about transplant surgery and blood transfusion.

Consider moral and religious teaching about transplant surgery and blood transfusion.

Key terms

Transplant surgery: when someone else's organs are put into a patient.

Blood transfusion: when a patient is given extra blood as part of an operation.

A *Dr Christiaan Barnard – pioneer heart surgeon, who performed the world's first heart transplant*

Some people refuse to carry a donor card primarily because they do not want to be buried or cremated 'incomplete'. This is sometimes linked to ideas about the afterlife. Muslims and Jews are reluctant to be donors because Islam and Judaism forbid 'desecrating or mutilating the body'. However, organ donation is often seen as the 'lesser of two evils' and so is permitted, because it enables life to be saved, which is an admirable thing to do.

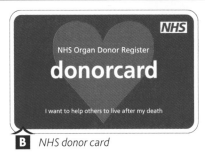

B *NHS donor card*

Discussion activity

2 a   Would you carry a donor card? Why?

   b   Some people are in favour of people carrying a 'non-donor card'. This would allow doctors to take organs from anybody *not* carrying this card. Why do you think they are in favour of this? Do you agree with them?

Beliefs and teachings

If anyone saved a life, it would be as if he saved the life of the whole people.

Qur'an 5:32

◼ Blood transfusion

Many operations require the patient to have their blood replaced, or more likely 'topped up', with blood from the same blood group. This is called a **blood transfusion**. Most people are in favour of this although Jehovah's Witnesses (a religious group associated with Christianity) refuse transfusions because they feel their life is carried in their blood so they cannot have anybody else's blood. This is an interpretation of Leviticus 17:11 – 'For the life of a creature is in the blood' – that other Christians do not share. It has resulted in several Jehovah's Witnesses dying in situations that have required a life-saving transfusion. Many transplants can be successfully carried out without a blood transfusion. Such 'bloodless transplants' are acceptable to Jehovah's Witnesses.

Study tip

Some candidates in examinations make incorrect statements about the Jehovah's Witness position on transplants and transfusion. Make sure, if you want to refer to them, that you have researched their belief and can write about it correctly.

SAVE A LIFE **GIVE BLOOD**
0845 7 711 711
www.blood.co.uk   BBC2 Ceefax page 465

C

Activity

Why do you think more people are in favour of blood transfusion than organ transplantation?

Summary

You should now be able to discuss transplant surgery and blood transfusion, and the moral issues associated with them.

What is human genetic engineering?

There is no doubt that science has made a huge contribution to all our lives and will continue to do so for as long as we live. However, some advances in science are controversial because people see them as 'tampering' with life itself. It seems that for every scientist developing new techniques or making new discoveries, there are many people pointing out moral or ethical reasons why the scientist's work should be opposed. There are often legal considerations as well, and this is certainly so in the scientific fields of **human genetic engineering** and **embryology**. Embryology means the study of **embryos** (fertilised eggs up to 14 days old) and human genetic engineering often, but not always, involves using human embryos.

Whilst few people would want to have the option to make choices like the ones in the cartoon, it is not impossible that, in the future, such a choice may be available. Indeed, American scientists working under government licence have already produced a genetically modified human embryo using technology that could lead to the selection of genes specifying height, intelligence and hair colour, for example. If allowed (it is currently illegal), this technology could lead to '**designer babies**', where parents could choose the gender and characteristics they would like their baby to have.

However, most scientists in the field of human genetic engineering are strongly opposed to using this technology for designer babies and insist that the purpose of their work on human embryos is to find ways of curing human diseases caused by faulty genes and to be able to select healthy, disease-free embryos to implant in a potential mother's womb. These embryos are produced by IVF treatment and then screened for faulty genes. If no faulty genes are found, the embryo can be implanted into the womb in the knowledge that the resultant baby will be free from genetic disease.

Objectives

Investigate the meaning of human genetic engineering and embryology.

Evaluate the effectiveness and morality of human genetic engineering and embryology.

Apply religious teachings to human genetic engineering and embryology.

Beliefs and teachings

He bestows [children] male or female according to His will.

Qur'an 42:49

A

So what is wrong with human genetic engineering?

For many people, there is nothing at all wrong with it. If human genetic engineering and embryology prevent disease and contribute to the birth of a healthy baby who will have a good quality of life, it must be good. However, some religious people think that it is encouraging scientists to take on the role of God the creator. In addition, many religious people are concerned about what happens to the unused embryos. IVF creates more embryos than are needed, but by law they must all be destroyed no later than 14 days after conception. For many people this is not a problem. However, for those who believe life begins at conception, it is a problem because it can be regarded as murder, which is illegal and against the teachings of all religions.

In May 2008, the British Parliament voted in favour of the *Human Fertilisation and Embryology Bill*, which is designed to make it clear just what is allowed by law and what is not. Cardinal Keith O'Brien, giving the Roman Catholic view, was quoted as saying that the bill is a 'monstrous attack on human rights, human dignity, and human life' which would allow experiments of 'Frankenstein proportion'. Whilst there are undoubtedly many Roman Catholics who agree with him, he was accused by some politicians and scientists of scaremongering and misleading the public by using emotive language and exaggerating the potential results of the research the Bill allows.

Key terms

Human genetic engineering: the modification of gene make-up to change the features of a human.

Embryology: the study of human embryos.

Embryo: fertilised ovum at about 12–14 days when implanted into the wall of the womb.

Designer babies: babies with gender and characteristics chosen by their parents, which is currently illegal.

Activities

1 From what you know and have read on this page, do you think Cardinal Keith O'Brien was correct in what he said? Why?

2 Should people have the chance to choose what their baby is like or should it be left to nature? Give your reasons.

Beliefs and teachings

I will not harm any living thing.

First Precept

Discussion activity

Discuss the case study below with a partner. Do you agree that the law should prevent embryos with genetic defects being selected for implantation or should couples have the right to choose?

Gene selection

Mr and Mrs Jones have both been deaf from birth. They want to have a child, but would prefer that child to be deaf. They asked their health authority to provide treatment that would allow an embryo containing a defective gene causing deafness to be selected and implanted into Mrs Jones' womb. Their request was turned down because even though it is possible, the Human Fertilisation and Embryology Act 2008 makes it illegal.

Case study

Summary

You should now be able to discuss the use and effectiveness of human genetic engineering and embryology, and the moral and religious issues associated with it.

Saviour siblings

If you had a brother or sister who was very ill, possibly even facing death, it is likely that you would do all you could to help them out or save their life.

You might feel differently if you had been born just for that reason. If a child is suffering from one of certain inherited diseases, the most compatible cure would be by transplanting **stem cells** from a sibling (sister or brother). The stem cells need to be collected from the sibling's umbilical cord, bone marrow or other tissue. This possibility is now offered by genetic technology on embryos and is legal in Britain under the Human Fertilisation and Embryology Act 2008. However, it is not legal to create a **saviour sibling** to donate organs, cells or tissues. A further issue is that unused embryos created for the purpose must be disposed of.

Discussion activity

Think of some reasons why people might oppose the idea of 'saviour siblings'. Compare your reasons with those of others in the class to compile a complete list.

What do religions say about genetic engineering?

Buddhism

Buddhists believe that the intention behind a deed (Right Intention) is important. If embryology is developed to save or improve life, it is acceptable. However, some Buddhists believe the cost in terms of the destruction of embryos is too great because it goes against the First Moral Precept not to kill a living thing. Others believe an embryo is not a fully embodied person because it does not possess the five Skandhas (form, feelings, perceptions, thoughts and consciousness).

Christianity

Many Christians oppose genetic engineering because it takes or devalues life. Church leaders – especially Roman Catholics – were opposed to the Human Fertilisation and Embryology Act 2008 and were keen to get their point across through various media. Their main arguments were based on the ideas of the 'sanctity of life' and that it is against the teachings of God for scientists to take on the role of creator or experiment on and dispose of living embryos. Whilst many fell short of calling this murder and therefore against the sixth of the Ten Commandments: 'You shall not murder' (Exodus 20:13, from the Bible), some did use this to justify their opposition.

Objectives

Further investigate human genetic engineering and embryology.

Evaluate the moral issues arising out of the creation of saviour siblings.

Consider religious teachings about human genetic engineering and embryology.

Key terms

Stem cell: a cell, most often taken from a 4–5 day-old embryo, whose role in the body is yet to be determined.

Saviour siblings: a sibling (brother or sister), genetically compatible with a sick child is implanted and born to use stem cells to treat the sick child.

Beliefs and teachings

If one speaks or acts with a wicked mind, unhappiness follows ... similarly, if one speaks or acts with a pure mind, happiness follows.

Dhammapada

Other Christians are in favour of genetic engineering because the positive aspects of helping each other and eradicating disease are truly loving and create a better quality of life. They believe God-given intelligence and creativity should be developed and used positively.

Hinduism

Hindus believe in ahimsa – not harming any living thing. However, if genetic engineering is for the reason of helping others, it may be allowed. Otherwise it is likely to promote bad karma, which makes it more difficult to escape samsara – the cycle of life, death and rebirth.

Islam

Ideas about the sanctity of life, disposal of unwanted embryos and the creator God are relevant to Muslims. However, there is some debate about when life begins – the unborn child does not receive a soul until 120 days (some muslims believe 40 days) after conception but this does not mean misuse of embryos is allowed. Allah has given us skills to help others and the development of genetic and embryo technology is an extension of this.

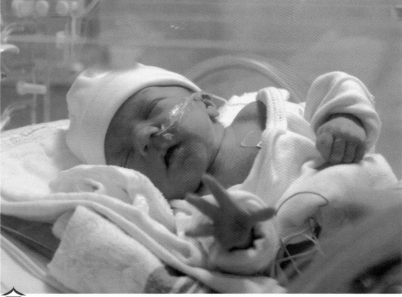

Judaism

Saving human life is important to Jews and, if genetic engineering achieves this, it is perhaps acceptable. However, embryos must be treated with respect. The ideas about the sanctity of life, disposal of unwanted embryos and the creator God also apply in Judaism.

 A *A critically ill baby*

Sikhism

God is the creator and an embryo is a person from conception. Spare embryos from IVF can be used, but only for genetic engineering designed to eliminate illnesses. However, some Sikhs believe that the cycle of birth, death and rebirth rules out human interference and so are against genetic and embryo technology.

Beliefs and teachings

A human person ... needs to be treated ... as an end in itself, not a tool for someone else's agenda.

Rowan Williams, *Archbishop of Canterbury*

Activities

1 Do you think that embryos are human beings? Explain your reasons.

2 Is 'You shall not murder' a good argument against genetic engineering? Identify another argument that could be used against it.

3 What arguments in favour of genetic engineering can you think of? Which are religious arguments?

4 Choose one of the six religions above. Write a paragraph explaining believers' opinions on genetic engineering.

Summary

You should now be able to discuss human genetic engineering and embryology in more depth, including saviour siblings. You should also be able to apply religious teachings to these issues.

Cloning – what is it?

Advances in genetic engineering have led to scientists developing techniques that some people find exciting and positive and with which others are uneasy, for either religious or non–religious reasons. One of these techniques is **cloning**, which is the creation of a genetically identical copy of an organism. Two main types of cloning are possible.

Reproductive cloning

This is the creation of an identical copy of an organism, which could be an animal, a plant or even a human (although creating a human clone in this way is illegal). Cloning has been common in selective animal breeding for many years. Most cloning involves separating cells in the very early stages of embryo development and then developing them into genetically identical organisms. Cloning came to widespread public attention in 1996 when scientists cloned 'Dolly' the sheep.

The idea that reproductive human cloning could provide an army of clones to take over the world is not realistic, as there are legal controls in place to prevent this from happening.

Therapeutic cloning

This is sometimes known as stem-cell cloning. The aim is to clone biological material to produce embryos from which stem cells can be taken and used in research to find treatments for a range of diseases. According to the law, once the embryo reaches 14 days from conception, it has to destroyed. Although the theory of therapeutic cloning is sound, scientists will need to do a great deal more work on developing the technique and thoroughly testing the results. This is likely to take many years.

Objectives

Gain knowledge and understanding of the concept of cloning.

Realise that there are different types of cloning.

Understand arguments for and against cloning.

Key terms

Cloning: the scientific method by which animals or plants can be created which have exactly the same genetic make-up as the original, because the DNA of the original is used.

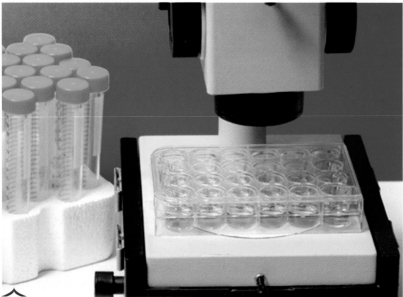

A *Can cloning ever be justified?*

What does the law say about cloning?

The law on cloning is complex. Although, in theory, the techniques employed in therapeutic cloning could lead to reproductive cloning by inserting the genetically identical embryo into a woman's uterus and allowing it to develop into a baby, it is illegal. Any laboratory involved in cloning is carefully licensed to ensure this cannot happen. However, the law has to keep pace with the science. Some non-scientists believe that scientists will continue to push the boundaries of what is legal and acceptable, and the law will have to catch up with these advances. That is what the Human Fertilisation and Embryology Act 2008 was designed for – updating the previous 1990 Act. Some say this is progress; others are worried that the boundaries are being pushed too far.

Study tip

If you are asked to answer a question on cloning, it might be appropriate to include something about both therapeutic and reproductive cloning.

Activities

1 Carefully explain the difference between reproductive cloning and therapeutic cloning.

2 Why does the law always seem to be trying to catch up with scientific advances?

B   *The law on cloning is complex*

To clone or not to clone?

There are many arguments for and against cloning. Some are specifically religious and connected with ideas about what is the most loving thing to do, acting from the right intention, the sanctity of life, God the creator, and the disposal of spare embryos (see previous page). Of course, religious people's opinions can be influenced by non-religious considerations as well as religious teachings. Therefore some religious people may believe that cloning is acceptable because:

- it helps with embryonic research, which could help sick or infertile people
- it is compassionate and improves people's quality of life
- people have a right to choose, and free will is God-given
- God inspires people to develop new technology to benefit mankind.

Other religious people may disagree because:

- it is against nature and against the way we were created by God
- it results in the disposal of many leftover embryos, which may be seen as individual humans or might otherwise grow into humans
- it may encourage scientists to make further advances that are even more unacceptable
- reproductive cloning affects a person's identity and position in the family
- a cloned person may not have a soul.

Beliefs and teachings

It is He [Allah] who created you from a single person.

Qur'an 7:189

Activity

3 'Cloning is always wrong.' Do you agree? Give reasons for your answer, showing you have thought about more than one point of view. Refer to religious arguments in your answer.

Summary

You should now be able to discuss the different types of cloning and their implications.

Should we experiment on humans or hybrids?

As science advances, some people's concerns about the morality of the possible results grow. Whilst some things (e.g. designer babies and reproductive cloning) are quite possible, the question 'Are they right?' is asked repeatedly. What is decided to be legally right or wrong is not necessarily morally right or wrong.

One such scientific advance is in experimenting on human beings in such a way as to produce **human-animal hybrid embryos**.

Objectives

Gain knowledge and understanding of experimenting on humans.

Evaluate the possible use of human experimentation.

Key terms

Human-animal hybrid embryo: an embryo made from human DNA and animal eggs for purposes of experimentation.

Human experimentation: testing products, usually medicines, on paid human volunteers.

Discussion activity

1   Who do you think should decide what is morally right or wrong – politicians, religious people, scientists, the general public or anybody else? Maybe a combination of some or all of these? Give reasons for your answer.

Human-animal hybrid embryos

In March 2008, scientists from Newcastle University announced that they had developed a part-human, part-animal embryo. They injected DNA from human embryo cells into eggs taken from the ovaries of a cow which had almost all their genetic material removed. These human-animal hybrid embryos survived for three days. The scientists hope that, in the future, they can produce similar embryos that survive for six or seven days in order to extract stem cells (the body's 'master cells') which will then be used in experiments to help find new treatments for conditions such as Parkinson's and Alzheimer's disease. Although this process is legal in Britain (it is illegal to keep the embryos for more than 14 days or implant them into a human or animal uterus), events at Newcastle University were criticised by religious leaders, who believed that it was against nature and the will of God.

Beliefs and teachings

Love your neighbour as [you love] yourself.

Luke 10:27–28; Leviticus 19:18

Discussion activity

2   Should the creation of human-animal hybrid embryos be legal? If so, would you include any conditions on their creation or use? If not, why not?

Research activity

Find out more about genetic engineering at **www.beep.ac.uk**

Human experimentation

Many people are very much against testing new drugs and cosmetics on animals to provide evidence that they are safe for humans to use. Some question whether such tests are reliable because animals have a different genetic make-up from humans. In order to make sure products are safe, the final level of testing is **human experimentation** – carrying out clinical trials on human volunteers. All human medicines are tested in this way. However, recently, some cancer drugs were licensed early because cancer sufferers wanted to use them regardless of the slight possibility of risk.

Whilst this form of testing is usually safe for the volunteers (who are paid for volunteering), there have been occasions when things have gone horribly wrong. In March 2006, six men suffered multiple organ failure within hours of taking the drug TGN1412 in a clinical test in London. The most seriously injured victim was in hospital for several months and had to have his toes amputated. Another was told by doctors he had the early indications of an aggressive form of cancer.

Stage 1 Laboratory testing

Tissue samples are tested in vitro and by computer simulation

Drug tested for toxicity on animals (mainly rodents)

Drug cleared for testing on humans by Medicines and Healthcare Products Regulatory Agency and other ethical bodies

Stage 2 Human testing

1 Drug tested for safety and side effects on healthy volunteers

2 Drug tested for effectiveness and side effects on selected people with relevant illness

3 Drug tested for full information on large numbers of people with relevant illness

Stage 3 Drug licensing

4 Drug tested more widely against other drugs, for side effects and long-term risks and benefits

🏠 *The process of testing drugs*

Activity

1 a You have been offered £2,000 to take part in a clinical trial. You have to take a course of tablets for two months and visit a clinic and be examined by a doctor every week. What would you do? Why?

b After you have made your decision, you hear that a person in Chicago has taken a similar course of tablets and been very ill (they have recovered). Would you change your decision? Give your reasons.

c The problem in Chicago encourages the company running the trial to increase the fee to £4,000. What would you do? Why?

d If you still wished to take part in the trial, are there any circumstances in which you would withdraw your services?

Beliefs and teachings

Do not do to another what you do not like to be done to yourself.

Mahabharata

Summary

You should now be able to discuss experimentation on humans and the moral issues associated with it.

What does religion say about matters of life?

When does life begin?

Activity

1 Without looking at the rest of this page, decide when you think life begins. You could tell your partner or class or have a vote, or your teacher might ask you to move to a certain part of the room to express your view.

This is the key question for a religious person to answer when reflecting on whether human fertility treatment is acceptable or not. From conception to birth is usually around 38 weeks and there are certain key points during that period that influence ideas about when life begins. Whatever anybody says, nobody can prove when life begins.

- **Before conception** – Buddhists, Hindus and Sikhs believe a pre-existing life force enters the body at conception.
- **Conception** – Some people believe a new life starts at conception because the sperm and egg are from a living source. This is a mainly Roman Catholic belief, although some other Christians and other people who don't believe in any religion agree with it.
- **14 days** (approximately) after conception the embryo becomes attached to the womb.
- **Three weeks** (approximately) after conception the heart begins to beat.
- **Quickening** – The first movements in the womb may be felt after about nine weeks.
- **Ensoulment** – Muslims believe the foetus gains a soul 120 days (around 19 weeks) after conception. Others may link this with development of the nervous system, brain activity or organ development at various other times.
- **Viability** – This is when the foetus could survive (with a great deal of medical help) if born prematurely. This occurs at about 24 weeks (the present upper limit for abortion, although in cases of profound disability abortion is allowed up to the time of birth).
- **Birth** – Jews (and others) believe human life starts at birth (about 38 weeks after conception). Until then, the baby is a foetus, totally dependent upon its mother.

Key terms

Conception: the moment the sperm fertilises the egg.

Quickening: the first detectable movements of the foetus.

Ensoulment: the belief that at one moment the foetus receives a soul (some believe it doesn't).

Viable: the point at which a foetus could survive if it were to be born.

Beliefs and teachings

You shall not murder.

Exodus 20:13

Beliefs and teachings

(Do not) take life – which Allah has made sacred – except for just cause.

Qur'an 17:33

Study tip

In response to evaluation questions that carry six marks, you need to evaluate two points of view that are sufficiently different, though not necessarily opposed, in order to gain top marks.

links

Look back to pages 20–23 to remind yourself of the issues involved in human genetic engineering.

Activity

2　a　After reading this information, have you changed your mind about when life begins?

　　b　When do you think life begins? Give reasons for your choice.

　　c　Choose another time from the list above. Write reasons why you think it is not when life begins.

　　d　Why do you think deciding when life begins is a key question when considering fertility treatment? Explain your reasons.

■ So how does this affect religious beliefs?

The first two stages on the timeline are the crucial ones that affect religious beliefs. If life starts at or before conception, fertility treatment, human genetic engineering and embryology involve taking life, something all religions oppose. However, religious people would also look at whether the taking of life, when it is at that stage only a tiny cluster of cells, will lead to developments and practices that will benefit individual people or the whole human race. If that is the case, the procedure might be seen as acceptable. For Buddhists, the idea of the right intention (from the Eightfold Path) would come into play, and for Buddhists, Sikhs and Hindus, the increasing of good karma is relevant. Jews, Christians and Muslims believe that in helping others through compassion, they are helping God.

It is interesting to note that 14 days is not only the 'age' at which the embryo becomes attached to the womb but it is also the 'age' after which embryos cannot be experimented on and have to be destroyed. If life begins after 14 days, religious arguments against such treatments are much weaker because by then genetic work is not allowed. However, even those who believe life starts well after 14 days do expect embryos to be treated with dignity and respect because they hold the potential for human life – something that is very special.

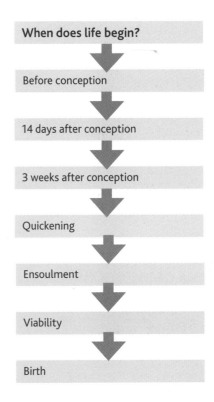

When does life begin?

Before conception

14 days after conception

3 weeks after conception

Quickening

Ensoulment

Viability

Birth

Activity

3　Reread this chapter, and pages 8–11, 22–23 and 28–29 especially carefully. Collect teachings for the religion or religions you are studying and write them into your books to provide a summary of what the religious believers you are studying believe.

links

Look back to pages 10–11 to remind yourself about why human life is special.

Extension activity

'It doesn't matter when life begins; if we have the technology to do things, we should do them.' What do you think?

Summary

You should now be able to discuss the concept of when life begins and apply religious teachings to matters of life.

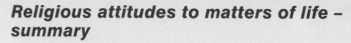

1

Religious attitudes to matters of life – summary

For the examination you should now be able to:

✔ understand and explain the concepts of 'sanctity of life', 'value of life' and 'quality of life'

✔ understand and discuss the debate about when life begins and how religious beliefs relate to that issue

✔ evaluate and discuss the moral issues involved in:

- fertility treatment
- surrogacy
- transplant surgery
- blood transfusion
- genetic engineering
- embryology
- cloning
- stem cell research
- experiments on humans.

✔ discuss religious teachings that relate to the topics above

✔ give at least one case study to illustrate the issues involved in the topics above

✔ discuss it from different points of view, including religious ones.

Sample answer

1 Write an answer to the following exam question:
'Matters of life are for religious people to sort out, not scientists.'
What do you think? Explain your opinion.
(3 marks)

2 Read the following sample answer:

> I disagree with this opinion. Scientists have done a lot of work and given childless people the chance to have a child. I think everybody deserves to be able to have a child and scientists make it possible. Science deals with facts anyway and so is much more important than religion. Science will achieve much more in the future than religion ever will.

3 With a partner, discuss the sample answer. Do you think that there are other things that the student could have included in the answer?

4 What mark would you give this answer out of 3? Look at the mark scheme in the Introduction on page 7 (AO2). What are the reasons for the mark you have given?

Practice questions

1   Look at the photograph below and answer the following questions.

(a) Explain briefly what is meant by 'in vitro fertilisation' (IVF).   *(2 marks)*

> **Study tip**
> You need to give a full explanation of the phrase, making either two points or a development of one point to show you understand the term.

(b) Explain why some religious people might be in favour of in vitro fertilisation (IVF).   *(3 marks)*

> **Study tip**
> Here you are asked to **explain**, so include some detail to show you understand the reasons why some religious people might be in favour.

(c) 'Religious believers should not use surrogacy.' What do you think? Explain your opinion.   *(3 marks)*

> **Study tip**
> Remember that even if you are asked for your opinion, you will actually get marks for the reasons you give. Try to write one well-developed reason or several simple ones, or a mixture of both.

(d) Give two reasons why a religious person might oppose artificial insemination by donor (AID).   *(4 marks)*

> **Study tip**
> When a question asks you to give two **reasons**, you will earn one mark for each reason (provided they are correct) and one mark for showing that you understand each one (four marks in total). If you give only one reason, you can gain a maximum of only two marks. Giving more than two reasons will not gain extra marks.

(e) 'It is God, and not people, who is in charge of matters of life.' Do you agree? Give reasons and explain your answer, showing you have thought about more than one point of view. Refer to religious arguments in your answer.   *(6 marks)*

> **Study tip**
> Note that the final question is worth the most marks and you will not be given any marks for simply agreeing or disagreeing. Before you start writing, think carefully of reasons why some people think God is in charge of matters of life and reasons why some people think people are in charge of matters of life. You will gain marks for making a judgement based on evidence, analysis and argument.

2.1 What is death?

Life and death

In the great scheme of things, our 'three score years and ten' (70 years) on an earth that has supported life for millions of years seem to be completely insignificant. Few make any lasting contribution that causes them to be remembered by society at large, but we all exist after **death** in the memories of those whom we know and love whilst we are here.

Activity

1 a With a partner, make a list of the ten greatest people who have ever lived. They must not be alive now.

  b Which of them is the greatest? Why?

  c Write a word after each person's name, to describe the way in which you think they became great, e.g. politics, religion, art, science, etc.

  d Which 'category' is most popular? Why do you think this is?

Key terms

Death: the end of life, which can be determined in several ways but normally when the brain stops functioning.

So what is death?

This seems to be a completely straightforward question with an obvious answer. Nothing could be further from the truth, however. Forty years ago, if your heart stopped beating, you were considered to have died. Now, brain death seems to be the main factor. The decision about whether someone is brain dead is made by checking that there is no eye movement, that the pupils in the eyes are fixed and dilated (larger than usual), and that there is no sign of breathing. It does not take into account whether or not the heart is beating. However, people who are brain dead can be kept 'alive' on a life-support machine, despite there being no prospect of 'life' as we know it, and they don't appear to be dead. Palliative care expert Professor Allan Kellehear has been quoted as saying:

> " Corpses are not warm, they are not pink, they do not move ... – but a person who is brain dead can be all of these things. "
>
> Professor Allan Kellehear

A A memorial stone aims to preserve the memory of loved ones

Beliefs and teachings

The dawn of a new day is the herald of a sunset. Earth is not our permanent home.

Guru Granth Sahib

However, at this point, a life-support machine can legally be turned off and death officially declared. It is also at this point that organs can legally be taken for transplant if the person or their family has given their consent.

Discussion activity ▪▪▪

1 a With a partner, try to agree your own definition of death.

b Did you find question **a** difficult? Explain why.

For a religious person, apart from a Buddhist, the definition of death would include the point at which the soul (spirit) leaves the body to begin an afterlife, whether that is in heaven or hell or being reborn or reincarnated in another body.

Extension activity

'R.I.P.' means 'rest in peace'. Explain what you think 'Rest in Peace' means.

B *Many people take comfort from being able to 'visit' their dead loved ones in a graveyard*

Important concepts about life and death

The three concepts of sanctity of life, value of life and quality of life are important when considering matters of death. In addition, beliefs about what happens after death (if anything) may influence a person's thoughts about matters to do with death when they are alive and affect their reactions and emotions when a person dies.

Beliefs and teachings

For God so loved the world that he gave his one and only Son, that whoever believes in him shall not perish but have eternal life.

John 3:16

Activity

2 a With a partner, discuss the following statement: 'When it is your turn to die, even if you are young, you die.'

b Now write about whether you agree with the statement. Give reasons for your opinion, showing that you have thought about more than one point of view.

Beliefs and teachings

When a person dies, the angels say 'What has he sent in advance?'

Muhammad

∞**links**

Revisit pages 10–11 to make sure you understand the concepts of sanctity of life, value of life and quality of life.

Beliefs and teachings

If one speaks or acts with a wicked mind, unhappiness follows ... similarly, if one speaks or acts with a pure mind, happiness follows.

Dhammapada

Study tip

When answering a six-mark AO2 question that asks you whether you agree and to give reasons, make sure you explain two different points of view. Remember, in giving your opinion, you cannot agree with both points of view.

Summary

You should now be able to discuss the problems to do with defining death and the importance of considering the sanctity of life, value of life and quality of life when thinking about issues of death.

2.2   Is death the end or a new beginning?

Is death the end?

Although less than 10% of the population of Britain worship regularly, over 90% have at least some religious element in their funeral. Often the ceremony will be led by a religious leader, prayers may be said and there may be a reading from a holy book relating to death and the afterlife.

Research activity

Find out more about what happens at a funeral in the religion(s) you are studying.

Discussion activity

With a partner, try to work out why most people prefer a religious funeral. Be prepared to share your ideas with others and write down the ones you think are the best.

Of course, there are many people who believe that once you are dead, there is nothing else. You live on only in the memories of those you knew and loved, and maybe in what you have achieved.

Death has always provoked sadness. In Victorian Britain, funerals became occasions for mourning the departed far more than ever before. Black was the predominant colour to symbolise mourning. Nowadays, whilst black is still the predominant colour at most funerals, some people ask those attending to wear bright colours, and funerals are more a celebration and remembrance of the person's life than a mourning of their death. This is a significant change.

Activity

1   'Funerals are more for the living than for the person who has died.' What do you think? Discuss your ideas with a partner and write a summary of the main points.

A new beginning

People have believed in life after death for thousands of years. Archaeologists have found Neanderthal burials all around Europe and Asia dating from over 25,000 years ago. Some of those people were buried with flowers, shells, animal teeth and other artefacts they thought might be important in the afterlife. The ancient Egyptians preserved the bodies of important people by mummifying them so they would be of use in the afterlife. Both customs were in place thousands of years before most of the major religions we know today had begun.

Objectives

Investigate beliefs about what happens after death.

Relate these beliefs to moral issues to do with death.

A   *John Lennon – whose music ensures he is not forgotten*

B   *An Egyptian mummy – preserved so that the body could be used in the afterlife*

The main religious beliefs about life after death

Heaven and hell

Jews, Christians and Muslims believe that when a person dies, God decides whether they should spend eternity in **heaven** (or paradise) with Him or in **hell** with the Devil. It depends very much on how they have followed their religion and how their beliefs have affected their actions throughout their life.

Muslims believe there is a 'state of waiting', called Barzakh, between death and the day of judgement. The dead will then enter paradise if Allah invites them to. Roman Catholics believe that there is a time of spiritual cleansing and preparation, called **purgatory**, for some before they enter heaven. Other Christians believe God chooses without the need for purgatory. There is, however, some discussion about whether the Day of Judgement that Jesus spoke of will be a future event when all are judged or an individual judgement when a person dies. Jewish belief, taken from the Talmud, talks about immediate entry into the 'world to come' being reserved for a small minority, with most having to wait for around a year so they can review their life and learn from their mistakes.

Christianity, Judaism and Islam all use powerful literal images, especially for hell. However, modern thinking suggests that heaven is a way of describing a state of being where God has an influence, whereas hell describes a state of being without God's influence.

Reincarnation and rebirth

Hindus, Sikhs and Buddhists believe in **reincarnation** or **rebirth**, which is dependent on good deeds (karma). They refer to samsara as being the cycle of birth, death and rebirth (Buddhism) or reincarnation (Hinduism and Sikhism). Hindus describe reincarnation as the soul discarding the body at death just as a person may take off clothes and put on new ones. Liberation from this cycle is called moksha. Sikhism believes the same. Buddhists do not believe in the soul or separate self (anatta) – at the time of rebirth, the impermanent life force that is fashioned by actions (karma) is reborn at a different level of life.

Whatever a person believes about life after death will affect their attitude to matters of death and death itself.

Study tip

If asked in the examination to give two different ideas about what happens after death, you could give heaven and hell for one idea and reincarnation or rebirth for the other, for example.

Activities

2   Write down what the religion(s) you are studying believe about life after death.

3   What do you think happens after death? Give reasons for your belief.

4   Why do you think beliefs about whether there is life or no life after death affect how people feel about death?

Extension activity

Why do you think Neanderthal man included artefacts in some burials?

Summary

You should now be able to discuss the way different religions explain death and what happens afterwards.

Attitudes to the elderly

The generation gap

Objectives

Understand some of the issues relating to the elderly.

Reflect on some of the problems faced by the elderly, including ageism.

Research activity

1. Try to find the lyrics of the song 'My Generation', written by Peter Townshend and sung by The Who. What does the first verse suggest to you about the generation gap between the young and the elderly?

Key terms

Ageism: prejudice and discrimination against the elderly.

The generation gap (difference in ideas and perceptions between people of different generations) has existed for many years. Young people still tend to think the elderly are old-fashioned and the elderly sometimes see young people as immoral and a potential threat to their safety. The comment 'It wasn't like that in my day' is often used by the elderly.

Discussion activities

1. Apart from your grandparents, how do you feel about the elderly? Give your reasons.

2. How do you think they feel about you as a young person? Give reasons.

Problems faced by the elderly

However, the perceived attitude of young people towards them is not the greatest problem the elderly face. There are many other potential problems.

- Many elderly people have to rely on a state pension and possibly state benefits. Poverty can be a real problem.

- There is an expectation that an elderly person will retire from all work and live on a pension. Many elderly people do not feel ready to retire and would prefer to work in order to keep their body and mind active. They may feel that their experience is undervalued and will be discarded. Others see retirement as a chance to do something different and less stressful during their remaining years.

- Illness can be more serious to the elderly than to younger people. They are more likely to have health problems caused by their age.

- They may become less mobile and more dependent on others to get around. As younger people have become more mobile, they may have moved away from where their elderly relatives live.

A *Many elderly people face more problems as they grow older*

- They may feel worthless to society because they are unable to make a contribution through paid work.

- They may face loneliness if their husband or wife dies. More than 2 million elderly people, most of them women, live alone. Some are housebound and dependent on health or social services to help them do what for others are simple tasks.

- The attitudes of others, including the media, can make the elderly feel that they are a burden on their families or on society in general.

Activities

1. With a partner, put the seven problems faced by the elderly in your own order of importance. Put the most important first and the least important last.

2. Explain your choice of the most and least important.

One in five people in Britain are over 65 years old, with around 2 million of them living alone. Whilst it is true that some of the elderly may face the problems listed above, many of them do not. Yet people's perceptions of them as being old and incapable of modern living may remain. This could be termed **ageism** – being 'pre-judged' to be inferior or less important because of their age.

People seem to forget that many elderly people grew up with the hardships imposed by war. At that time fathers and brothers joined the armed forces with the expectation that they probably wouldn't return and people constantly faced the fear of death or injury as bombs rained down on their communities. Many elderly people also faced other challenges, such as bringing up a family and providing food, clothing and a home for them.

Such experiences in their early years must have affected an elderly person's outlook on life and perhaps has given them a sense of realism in their expectations. Coupled with the wisdom they have gained through what they have experienced, the elderly have a lot to give to people facing the same kinds of pressure today.

B *Many people who have experienced the hardships of war have a particular perspective on life*

Beliefs and teachings

Respect your father and your mother so that you will live a long time in the land I am giving you.

Exodus 20:12

Research activity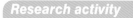

2. Using the internet or by asking older people you know, find out how much the basic state pension is.

Activities

3. What do you think can be done to help to make the lives of the elderly better?

4. Are the opinions of the elderly worth listening to? Give reasons for your answer.

5. What do you think the word 'wisdom' means?

Study tip

If you use a quotation in the examination, it is a good idea to say whom you are quoting, although it is not essential.

Summary

You should now be able to discuss the problems that face the elderly and how they feel about them and some of the benefits their experience can bring to living in the 21st century.

Discussion activity 👤👤👤

Spend two minutes talking with your partner about what is being said in the cartoon. What do you think the husband and wife are thinking? How do you feel about the situation?

What are the options?

While some elderly people are able to take care of themselves for the whole of their lives, many need to be cared for as they get older. This care can be provided by individuals or by a number of institutions. Many are cared for in their own home or the home of a family member. Some care is provided by local authorities (although it has to be paid for) and others rely on the support of charities or volunteers.

Living at home

Many elderly people are strongly independent and prefer to live in their own home, with support. The local social services may allocate a social worker to them or arrange for someone to help with the housework, perhaps at a small cost. They also may arrange for a hot meal to be delivered every day by the meals on wheels service, again at a small cost. If family live close by, they may visit regularly. However, if they have moved away for some reason, they may have to rely on the phone or neighbours and visit only on special occasions.

Living with family

Many families prefer to have elderly members of their family living with them. Indeed, this is a feature of the extended family favoured by Muslims among others. The ideal situation is when the elderly person is treated as an important member of the family, not as someone who lives there because there is no other option.

Teachings from some religions encourage this out of gratitude, respect and recognition of the wisdom the elderly possess. However, some would interpret such teachings as telling people to find the most appropriate way of caring for their elderly parents and this may rule out living with the family.

Objectives

Investigate alternative ways of caring for the elderly.

Apply religious teachings to caring for the elderly.

Beliefs and teachings

Honour your father and mother.

Exodus 20:12

SHE'S YOUR MOTHER – YOU DECIDE WHERE SHE LIVES.

A

Community options

Some elderly people move into sheltered housing, where they may rent a small flat within a complex of similar flats with a communal area for socialising. These are adapted to make them easier for elderly people to use, with a warden on duty to help the residents and take charge in an emergency. It allows elderly people to have some independence and privacy in a place they can call their own.

Residential homes for the elderly provide security and care when people are no longer easily able to look after themselves. Residents usually have their own room, but have use of a communal lounge and dining room. Meals are provided and some activities are often arranged so that people can socialise if they wish to.

Elderly people who are unwell may move into a care home, or a hospital for short-term treatment, where they have access to the medical care they need. If an elderly person has a terminal illness and is close to death, they may spend their final days or weeks in a hospice.

Beliefs and teachings

Having supported me, I will support them.

Sigalovada Sutta

Beliefs and teachings

May his nose be rubbed in dust who found his parents approaching old age and lost his right to enter paradise because he did not look after them.

Hadith

links

See pages 50–51 for more information on hospices and an explanation of the term.

Activity

1 a Which (if any) of the options for care (in the home, family or community) do you think is best? Explain why you think so.

   b Which of the options is your least favourite? Explain your reasons.

Extension activities

1 What special features do you think an elderly person might need in a sheltered housing flat? Give your reasons.

2 Design a one-bedroom flat suitable for an elderly person.

Deciding where to live

Joan is 86 years old. Her husband, Trevor, died three years ago after suffering a massive heart attack. Joan is finding it increasingly difficult to live in the home that she and Trevor shared for 33 years. She has arthritis and struggles to walk. She also has high blood pressure, which worries her. She feels she can no longer live at home and is prepared to sell her house to finance the rest of her life whilst hopefully having some money left to give to her daughter, Julie. Julie's husband, Robert, would like Joan to live in a residential home for the elderly, preferably one that is not too expensive. Julie would like her mother to come to live with her and Robert, especially now their own daughter has married and left home.

Case study

Study tip

When referring to any of these ways of looking after the elderly, these terms (e.g. sheltered housing) will help you.

Activity

2 In groups of four, role-play a conversation between Joan, Julie and Robert in the case study – and also include Sylvia, a social worker who has supported Joan for two years. Decide who takes which role, and prepare your conversation. Be prepared to perform your conversation for the class.

Summary

You should now be able to explain different ways of caring for the elderly, including the options encouraged by religion.

What religion teaches about the elderly

What does religion say about caring?

All religions teach that people should treat others with care and respect. 'Love your neighbour' is a Jewish teaching from Leviticus 19:18 that Jesus encouraged Christians to follow, and Buddhists and Hindus believe that you should not harm any living being (ahimsa – Hinduism; First Precept – Buddhism).

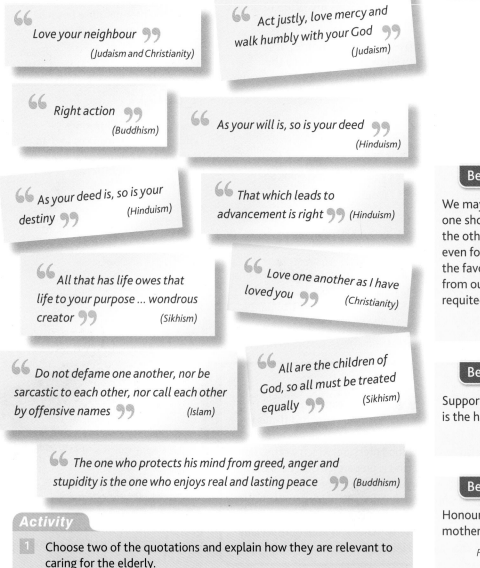

> Love your neighbour
> *(Judaism and Christianity)*

> Act justly, love mercy and walk humbly with your God
> *(Judaism)*

> Right action
> *(Buddhism)*

> As your will is, so is your deed
> *(Hinduism)*

> As your deed is, so is your destiny
> *(Hinduism)*

> That which leads to advancement is right
> *(Hinduism)*

> All that has life owes that life to your purpose ... wondrous creator
> *(Sikhism)*

> Love one another as I have loved you
> *(Christianity)*

> Do not defame one another, nor be sarcastic to each other, nor call each other by offensive names
> *(Islam)*

> All are the children of God, so all must be treated equally
> *(Sikhism)*

> The one who protects his mind from greed, anger and stupidity is the one who enjoys real and lasting peace
> *(Buddhism)*

Beliefs and teachings

We may carry our mothers on one shoulder and our fathers on the other and attend for them even for a hundred years ... still the favour we have received from our parents will be far from requited.

Anguttara Nikaya

Beliefs and teachings

Support for one's parents ... this is the highest protection.

Maha-Mangala Sutta

Beliefs and teachings

Honour your father and your mother.

Fifth Commandment, Exodus 20:12

Activity

1   Choose two of the quotations and explain how they are relevant to caring for the elderly.

What do religions say about the elderly?

Buddhism

The elderly are respected for their wisdom and experience. Some Buddhist care organisations help to care for the elderly, offering support for all their needs, including spiritual needs. However, the elderly person's children have a responsibility to look after them, which should be seen as a privilege. Buddhists believe in anicca (impermanence) and, because they may be ill or nearing death, the elderly are a good example of this. Looking after one's parents also provides an opportunity to gain good karma.

Christianity

Christians should support the elderly because they should be respected and are vulnerable. Traditionally, Christians have preferred to allow the elderly to keep their independence, but where this is not possible it is a duty to consider options carefully in order to provide the best for them, including the possibility of looking after them themselves. Churches provide facilities for the elderly and pastoral support, including regular Holy Communion at home or in a residential care home.

Hinduism

One of the five daily duties (Pitri Yajna) is to serve and care for parents and the elderly, who make up one of five sections of society given special respect. Parents are part of the extended family and, being very important, should be cared for, respected and obeyed throughout their lives. The eldest son is responsible for taking care of elderly parents, as he is considered the head of the family and takes a leading role at his parent's funeral. In addition, caring for the elderly earns good karma which helps in the goal of escaping samsara and thereby attaining moksha.

Islam

Islam has an extended family society, which means different generations of a family often live together. Elderly parents have the right to expect their children to care for them and it is the responsibility and duty of the whole family to do this because of the effort and sacrifices the parents have made and for the wisdom they have acquired throughout their life. Looking after the elderly provides spiritual growth. Sending elderly parents to a home is seen as unkind and disrespectful.

Judaism

In addition to the Fifth Commandment, Jews are also told to 'show respect for the elderly' (Leviticus 19:32). Jewish families are encouraged to look after the elderly through the extended family although it is acknowledged that this is not always possible. Therefore the Jewish community provides specialist homes for the very elderly and frail whose families lack the skills to support them. However, the wisdom of the elderly is valued.

Sikhism

Sikhs believe it is the duty of sons to look after their parents. This obligation is also seen as a service (sewa). In order to assist the family, the Sikh community often offers day care to the elderly in the Gurdwara. Homes for the elderly are rarely used and members of the extended family often live together.

Beliefs and teachings

Let your mother be a god to you. Let your father be a god to you.

Taittiriya Upanishad 1:11:2

Beliefs and teachings

The Lord hath decreed that ye be kind to parents.

Qur'an 17:23

Beliefs and teachings

Child, why do you quarrel with your father due to whom you have grown to this age? It is a sin to argue with him.

Guru Granth Sahib

Activity

2   a   Explain the reasons the religion(s) you are studying give for looking after the elderly, including elderly members of the family.

    b   Do you agree with these reasons? Explain why.

Study tip

Make sure you know what the religion you are studying teaches about care for the elderly and learn at least one quotation.

Summary

You should now be able to discuss why people should treat the elderly with respect, including for their wisdom and experience of life.

Should we be able to take life?

Taking life

With a partner, discuss the circumstances, if there are any, in which you think taking human life is justified.

In most circumstances, there would seem to be no reason at all why anybody should take life. However, if that were the case, there would be no war, no discussion about executing criminals and no murder. Those who support the idea of war, for example, would point out that fighting a war to defend your country against a hostile enemy is the right thing to do, even though it involves killing and possibly being killed. They believe that the cause is sufficient to justify the killing. But does that mean that a life taken in war is of less value than a life taken in other circumstances?

In the Jewish scriptures (Old Testament), the Sixth Commandment says 'You shall not murder' (Exodus 20:13) and the book of Leviticus takes it further by saying 'If anyone takes the life of a human being, he must be put to death' (Leviticus 24:17). This introduces the idea of illegal killing (murder) and legal killing (execution). Many people today support executing a person found guilty of murder. One of the reasons they give is to prevent the murderer from killing anyone else. Yet the end product is the same: someone dies, in this case the murderer along with the victim.

All religions condemn illegal killing but many believers think that legal killing is sometimes necessary. But Buddhists, in particular, are reluctant to engage in any killing, even in war. It is likely that others would investigate the circumstances before deciding.

A *Right or wrong?*

Objectives

Reflect on whether anyone has the right to take life.

Beliefs and teachings

Do not do to another what you do not like to be done to yourself.

Mahabharata

∞ links

Revisit pages 10–11 to make sure you understand the concepts of sanctity of life, value of life and quality of life.

Activities

1. Is it ever right to kill another person? Explain why/why not, giving some examples of situations in which you think it is right or wrong.

2. Is the life of a murderer worth less than the life of an innocent person? Explain your reasons.

3. Is the life of an enemy soldier worth less than the life of a soldier fighting on your side? Explain your reasons.

But who decides?

In the cases of execution (illegal in all countries in the European Union, including Britain) and war, the government has the power to decide to allow one person to kill another. But some people argue that no government has the right to allow this, whatever the circumstances.

This raises the questions of who, if anybody, should have the right to decide to end a person's life and whether actively ending a person's life is any different from allowing a person to die. The second question is one that doctors face on a regular basis. This situation is made more difficult if the person has made no secret of the fact that they would actually prefer to die rather than live in pain.

All the main religions, except Buddhism, believe that only God can make the decision of who dies and when. However, if this is true, it does not help us to decide whether taking life in war is how God intends a person to die. It does mean that if a person takes their own life or allows their life to be taken, they are sinning against God and running the risk of an afterlife without God or earning bad karma.

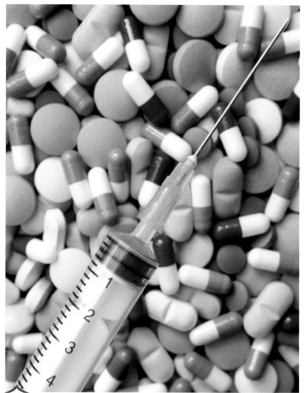

B *Kill or cure?*

∞ links

See pages 44–47 for more on euthanasia.

Activity

4 Do you think governments should have the right to allow a person to kill? Explain your reasons.

5 Who, if anybody, do you think has the right to allow a person to kill? Explain your reasons.

6 What do you think is the difference between ending life and allowing a person to die?

Why can you kill me when I am here for killing someone else?

Study tip

In the examination, you will not be asked a question on war or execution in this topic (although execution may appear in topic 4), but it is useful to consider how death in these circumstances differs from allowing a person to die through euthanasia.

Summary

You should now be able to discuss what religion teaches about taking life, including circumstances when it might be acceptable.

The euthanasia debate

The right to live?

In the 4th century BCE, the Greek doctor Hippocrates wrote the hippocratic oath, which he believed contained good moral guidance for doctors. It contains the following passage which assured patients that their life would be respected and protected:

> 66 *I will prescribe for the good of my patients according to my ability and my judgment and never do harm to anyone. To please no one will I prescribe a deadly drug nor give advice which may cause his death.* 99
>
> *Hippocrates*

For many years, this oath was sworn by doctors upon entering the profession. However, in Britain, it has largely been replaced by a statement of good medical practice issued by the General Medical Council. According to this, a good doctor will:

> 66 *Listen to patients and respond to their concerns and preferences ... Respect patients' right to reach decisions with you about their treatment and care.* 99
>
> *General Medical Council*

Discussion activity

1 What important differences in respect of life and death are there between the statements by Hippocrates and by the General Medical Council? Why do you think these changes have been made?

A right to die?

The word '**euthanasia**' means 'a gentle death' and is often referred to as 'mercy killing'. The intention of euthanasia is to assist a person who is suffering and perhaps close to death by giving them sufficient medication to kill them. As an act of compassion this will prevent them from suffering any further whilst possibly shortening their life by a few days or weeks. However, in Britain euthanasia is illegal because it could be seen as assisting someone to take their own life (suicide), which is in breach of the Suicide Act 1961. Others believe that people have a right to self-determination and they should have some control over when their own life ends.

Objectives

Investigate the meaning of euthanasia.

Evaluate whether euthanasia should be used.

Key terms

Euthanasia: inducing a painless death, by agreement and with compassion, to ease suffering. From the Greek meaning 'good death'.

Beliefs and teachings

Don't you know that you yourselves are God's temple and that God's Spirit lives in you? If anyone destroys God's temple, God will destroy him.

1 Corinthians 3:16–17

A Should people have the right to decide when to die?

2 Discuss Picture A. Is it a good representation of euthanasia? Explain what you think.

3 Should very ill people have the right to die? Discuss this with a partner. Then write down your thoughts.

There are three types of euthanasia. All are illegal in Britain, but the first two types of euthanasia are performed in some countries:

- voluntary – the person asks a doctor to end their life
- non-voluntary – the person is too ill to ask but it is believed to be in their best interests
- involuntary – as happened in Nazi Germany, disabled and sick people were killed without consultation.

If euthanasia happens, it can be passive or active:

- passive – this is either where the dose of a pain-killing drug, such as morphine, is increased in the belief that it will not only control pain but also shorten life, or where treatment is withheld or withdrawn because all it is doing is delaying the natural process of dying. Some say that this is not really euthanasia at all
- active – withholding treatment with the deliberate intention of ending life or giving a drug that will end life.

Activities

1 a Think of reasons why some people may be against euthanasia and reasons why others may be in favour of it.

   b Compare your ideas with your partner's.

   c Write down your ideas, adding any your partner has thought of that you haven't.

2 'Passive euthanasia is not really euthanasia at all.' What do you think? Explain your opinion.

Study tip

If writing about euthanasia, try to use the different types where appropriate and refer to either passive or active euthanasia.

Extension activity

Euthanasia is illegal in Britain, yet there are cases in which passive euthanasia has happened without the doctor being prosecuted. Spend some time thinking about this and write down your thoughts.

Some people decide to make a 'living will'. Whilst not legally binding, this is a document that sets out a person's wishes regarding the types of treatment they would like carried out if, in the future, they are incapable of making a decision.

Research activity 🔍

Find out more about living wills. Go to www.direct.gov.uk and search for 'living wills'.

Summary

You should now be able to discuss the different types of euthanasia and some of the issues concerning the topic.

2.8 Euthanasia – a case study

Background

Euthanasia is illegal in Britain. But it is legal in the Netherlands, Belgium and Switzerland, where there are safeguards to ensure that it is voluntary and that the person is in severe pain or that death is imminent. It allows a person to choose a dignified death.

The Swiss organisation Dignitas offers euthanasia for those suffering severe pain or terminal illness. Swiss law permits euthanasia if those assisting the death are not motivated by self-interest – they must not use it to get rid of a partner as a matter of convenience or to acquire a large sum of money. People in other countries now see Dignitas as a means of relieving their own suffering by euthanasia and of dying with dignity.

Case study

Reginald Crew

Reginald Crew, a 74-year-old from Liverpool, suffered from motor neurone disease for four years. It is a progressive disease that destroys motor neurones – the cells that control voluntary muscle activity, including breathing and other movement. This leads to weakness and the wasting-away of muscles, loss of mobility and eventually the inability to breathe. Many sufferers keep their mental capabilities and fully realise what is happening. There is no known cure. Some sufferers die within a year of contracting the disease but some, such as Professor Stephen Hawking, live with it for many years.

On New Year's Eve 2002, Reginald gave a moving interview to his local radio station. He explained that he was losing the use of his limbs and before long would not be able to communicate. He intended to end his life, but did not want anybody to get into trouble for assisting him. Therefore he had arranged to fly to Switzerland so that he could die with dignity assisted by Dignitas.

On 20 January 2003, after doctors were satisfied that he was in the correct mental state to make the decision, they agreed for him to be provided with a fatal dose of barbiturates in a drink. Reginald took the drink in the presence of his wife and daughter, and peacefully passed away. No legal action was taken.

DIGNITAS
To live with dignity
To die with dignity

A *Reginald Crew with his wife, Win*

Religious views

No religion officially supports euthanasia, although believers would not wish to see people suffering unnecessarily and would support the giving of pain relief.

Buddhism

Euthanasia is wrong and creates bad karma because it breaks the First Precept not to harm any living thing. Suffering is a fact of life that must be accepted. However, it could be argued that if the intention is merciful, it could be allowed.

Christianity

Christians usually disagree with euthanasia because of their belief in the sanctity of life, preferring to trust in God's mercy. Some, however, cannot believe that a loving God would want His people to suffer. They might argue that God-given freewill and intelligence give a person the right to choose to end their life when its quality is greatly reduced.

Hinduism

Hindus believe in ahimsa so euthanasia is not allowed. Suffering is believed to be the result of bad karma from a previous life, so it must be accepted.

Islam

Only Allah can take life, so euthanasia is therefore against His plan. However, passive euthanasia may be regarded as compassionate and not true euthanasia because it enables nature to take its course, whilst relieving pain.

Judaism

Life is God-given and a blessing that must be treasured. Because God gives life, only He should take it away.

Sikhism

Only God can give and take life and suffering is part of His plan. Euthanasia interrupts the plan and so is not allowed. However, according to some Sikhs, the quality of life is also important and may justify euthanasia in certain cases.

> **Beliefs and teachings**
>
> I will not harm any living thing.
>
> *First Precept*

> **Beliefs and teachings**
>
> You shall not murder.
>
> *Exodus 20:13*

Activities

3 Note down the beliefs of the religion you are studying that are relevant to euthanasia.

4 Do you think there is ever a good reason for euthanasia? If so, what is it? If not, why not?

Summary

You should now be able to discuss why euthanasia may or may not be a good thing and what religions teach about it.

2.9 How long should we keep people alive?

The use of life-support machines

A **life-support machine** allows a person to remain alive by assisting or replacing breathing in the hope that the person will recover and be able to breathe normally again. Without it the person would probably die. Life support also includes feeding by passing fluids (including essential mineral salts, glucose and water) through a tube directly into the stomach.

Case study

Tony Bland – victim of the Hillsborough disaster

On 15 April 1989, Tony Bland, an 18-year-old Liverpool football fan, travelled to the Hillsborough Stadium in Sheffield to watch his team play Nottingham Forest in an FA Cup semi-final. Tragically, just before the game kicked off, there was a surge of supporters who were in an area of the ground where everybody was standing. As a result, hundreds of supporters were injured in the crush, some very seriously, and 95 men, women and children lost their lives. One of the most seriously injured was Tony Bland, who was taken to hospital unconscious.

Tony had crushed ribs and two punctured lungs, which interrupted the supply of oxygen to his brain. As a result, his brain was irreversibly damaged and he was left in a 'persistent vegetative state' (PVS). His brain stem remained intact, but other areas of his brain showed no activity. Although there appeared to be no hope of recovery, Tony was kept alive on a life-support machine and fed through tubes.

It took until November 1992 for the family and Airedale NHS Trust, who were treating Tony, to overcome moral objections and legal difficulties and receive a court's permission to stop feeding him. This would allow him to die with some dignity and without his doctor facing a charge of murder. A further delay occurred whilst the legal decision was appealed in the House of Lords. However, on 22 February 1993, with permission having been gained, feeding was withdrawn and Tony Bland's life-support machine was switched off. Tony Bland finally died on 3 March 1993 – the 96th victim of what became known as the Hillsborough disaster.

A *The funeral of Tony Bland – victim of the Hillsborough disaster*

Discussion activity

1. a. With a partner, discuss who you think should have been allowed to make the final decision to let Tony Bland die.
   b. Do you think the correct decision was made in the end? Explain your reasons.
   c. Write down the results of your discussions.

Other ways of keeping people alive

In addition to a life-support machine, there are other ways of keeping people alive ranging from simple medicines that control otherwise serious conditions, such as diabetes and epilepsy, to 'hi-tech' equipment in hospital used by well-trained and caring medical staff. If a heart stops, it can be restarted with no after-effects and people recover from serious surgery that even a decade ago would not have been possible.

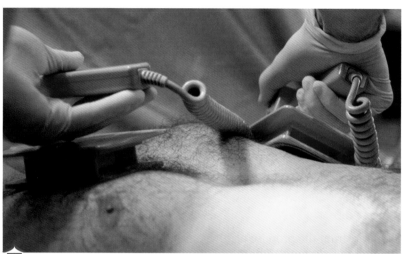

B *Defibrillation – an electric shock to start a heart that has stopped beating*

Religious and moral teachings

Advances in medical technology cause religious and moral thinkers to constantly update their beliefs and ideas. They use the same principles, such as:

- compassion
- quality of life
- sanctity of life
- the idea of causing no harm to any living thing
- using God-given talents and skills to save life.

All religions support turning off life-support machines for people who are brain dead. Although they recognise that this may be interpreted as taking God's role in life and death, they would prefer not to keep people alive with little prospect of a decent quality of life, *purely* to prolong it.

Research activity

Using the Internet and/or the library, find out more about the principles of compassion, quality of life, sanctity of life, causing no harm to any living thing and using God-given talents and skills to save life.

Activities

1 'Life should be prolonged regardless of its potential quality.' What do you think? Give your reasons.

2 Which of the five principles above do you think is most important when considering matters of life or death? Why?

Key terms

Life-support machine: a machine that keeps people alive when they would otherwise die.

Beliefs and teachings

Nor take life – which Allah has made sacred – except for just cause.

Qur'an 17:33

Beliefs and teachings

I myself am He! There is no god besides me. I put to death and I bring to life, I have wounded and I will heal, and no one can deliver out of my hand.

Deuteronomy 32:39

Summary

You should now be able to discuss the use of life-support machines and other methods of keeping people alive, as well as religious and moral dilemmas about whether a person should be allowed to die.

2.10   Help for the dying and bereaved

Can religion help the dying and bereaved?

Activity

1 'There's no point following a religion all your life because to get to heaven you just have to say sorry to God and he will forgive you.' What do you think about this statement? Write down your thoughts.

Christianity, Islam and Judaism teach that there is an afterlife in heaven with God, and this can be a comfort to those who are dying and to the bereaved, who are left behind. Those who follow their faith throughout or for much of their life, and who sincerely ask for God's forgiveness, will achieve this reward. In this way death becomes the beginning of something new and better, building on the faith and closeness to God established in this life. However, this type of relationship with God usually begins earlier in life and so a deathbed apology might be questioned for its sincerity. Followers believe that God or Allah knows our motives and whether we are being sincere or not.

Buddhists, Hindus and Sikhs may gain comfort from the promise of reincarnation or rebirth. However, a believer can only hope to be reincarnated or reborn to a better level of life if they have earned good karma by doing good deeds throughout their life.

Discussion activity

'If you don't follow a religion, you should not be allowed a religious funeral.' With a partner, discuss both sides of this argument. Without writing a speech, be prepared to present a case for either side to the rest of the class. Look back at pages 34 and 35, which may help you.

On a more practical level, religious people will be keen to support a dying person and their family. Religious leaders from within the community are also available to help if asked. Once the person has died, most bereaved people also need support before and during the funeral and in the weeks and months after it. They are **mourning**. For many people, the difficulties of coping without the person they love, perhaps on their own, can be a major problem.

Activity

2 Explain how a person, whether religious or not, could help someone who is struggling to cope with living on their own after their partner has died.

Objectives

Evaluate how religion may help the dying and bereaved.

Understand the contribution made by hospices.

Key terms

Mourning: a period of time which signs of grief are shown.

Hospice: a special place to which people go to die with dignity.

Sorry if you think I did anything wrong, God. I'll see you later –

A

Beliefs and teachings

I am the resurrection and the life. He who believes in me will live, even though he dies.

John 11:25

The hospice movement

In 1967, Dame Cicely Saunders set up St Christopher's in Sydenham, London – the first **hospice**. Her aim was to provide care for patients that considered their physical, spiritual, emotional and psychological well-being as a complete package rather than separately, as had been the case previously. Although hospices are not specifically religious places, Dame Cicely acknowledged her Christian beliefs as the main motivation for her work. Before she died, she said she would hope for a sudden death but would prefer a slower death that allowed her time to reflect on her life and to put her practical and spiritual affairs in order. In June 2005, she died of breast cancer in St Christopher's Hospice, the hospice she founded.

Hospices are good examples of one way in which people can provide help for the dying. Patients receive palliative care – sufficient pain relief to maintain relative comfort and consciousness. Pastoral support can be arranged and the patient's other needs are also met so that they, their friends and their family can prepare for their imminent death. They can die with dignity in a familiar place, probably in the presence of loved ones. Hospices also give practical support and comfort to the friends and relatives of the dying.

There are hospices that specialise in looking after children, where their specific needs and the needs of their families can be better catered for. The emphasis there is not only on preparing for death but also on encouraging the child to enjoy their last months and weeks doing many of the sorts of thing that most children normally do.

> **Beliefs and teachings**
>
> We do not become saints or sinners by words or by saying that we are. It is our actions repeated over and over that are engraved on our soul.
>
> *Japji Sahib* prayer

B *Dame Cicely Saunders, founder of the hospice movement*

Research activity

Go to the website **www.stchristophers.org.uk** to find out more about the hospice movement.

Activities

3   Explain what a hospice is.

4   In your opinion, is a hospice or passive euthanasia the best way to help a terminally ill person in the last few days of their life? Say why.

5   Hospices rely mainly on charity for their funding. Do you think they should be funded out of general taxation? Try to think of reasons for each possible point of view.

6   Are there any other ways religion can help the dying and their families?

> **Study tip**
>
> Do not confuse a hospice with a hospital or a hostel.

> **Summary**
>
> You should now be able to discuss the help and comfort offered by hospices and religion to the dying and bereaved.

2

Religious attitudes to the elderly and death – summary

For the examination you should now be able to:

✔ understand and explain the term 'death'

✔ discuss religious beliefs about what happens after death

✔ understand the problems faced by the elderly and discuss what younger generations might learn from them

✔ discuss the options of care for the elderly and religious teachings on the topic

✔ understand the law relating to death and euthanasia

✔ evaluate the debate on euthanasia and whether anyone has the right to take life

✔ evaluate the circumstances in which the use of a life-support machine should be discontinued

✔ discuss religious teachings that relate to allowing someone to die

✔ describe the provision of care in the community for the elderly and the dying

✔ understand and explain the ways religion can help the dying and bereaved

✔ give real-life examples to support your points

✔ discuss topics from different points of view, including religious ones.

Sample answer

1 Write an answer to the following exam question:
   Give two reasons why a religious person might support the hospice movement.

   (4 marks)

2 Read the following sample answer:

   > A religious person would support the hospice movement because hospices allow people to die with dignity, which shows the compassionate and loving side of religion – "love your neighbour". They also don't use euthanasia.

3 With a partner, discuss the sample answer. Do you think that there are other things that the student could have included in the answer?

4 What mark would you give this answer out of 4? Look at the mark scheme in the Introduction on page 7 (AO1). What are the reasons for the mark you have given?

Practice questions

1   Look at the photograph below and answer the following questions.

(a) Explain briefly the meaning of 'ageism'.   *(2 marks)*

Study tip Even though you are not asked to, you could give an example if you think it might help you to explain the word.

(b) Explain why some religious people might want to avoid putting an elderly relative in a residential home for the elderly.   *(3 marks)*

Study tip Try to include at least one religious teaching to support the reasons you are giving.

(c) 'Elderly people from religious families should be looked after by their families.' What do you think? Explain your opinion.   *(3 marks)*

Study tip Note that this question does not ask for more than one point of view.

(d) Give two reasons why a religious person might be against euthanasia.   *(4 marks)*

Study tip If you give only one reason, you can gain a maximum of only two marks. Giving more than two reasons will not gain extra marks.

(e) 'Beliefs about life after death don't matter when considering how to look after the dying.' Do you agree? Give reasons and explain your answer, showing you have thought about more than one point of view. Refer to religious arguments in your answer.   *(6 marks)*

Study tip Remember to use religious beliefs and teachings to support the points you are making in answer to the final question – don't just state that it is what some people believe.

3.1 Introduction

■ What is a drug?

A **drug** is a substance that can be natural or manufactured in a laboratory, which if introduced into the body has an effect on the way the mind and body work. The effects could be beneficial in preventing, controlling or curing illness, provided that the drug is used in the way intended by the manufacturer or the doctor who has prescribed it.

But there are dangers associated with drugs. Many of the more powerful ones are **prescription drugs**, which can only be prescribed by a doctor. Accidental overdoses, whether of prescribed drugs or of over-the-counter drugs such as painkillers, can be fatal. This is a particular risk if children get hold of drugs and take them thinking that they are sweets. Deliberate overdoses of prescribed drugs or painkillers are also used by people intending to take their own lives. However, despite being a very serious problem, these examples of the misuse of drugs are only the tip of a very large iceberg.

■ Drug abuse

Of course, the availability of drugs can lead to **drug abuse**. Prescribed drugs that are intended as stimulants or depressants for people with psychological problems can have devastating effects if taken by people for whom they are not prescribed, taken to excess or taken with other drugs such as alcohol. Others fall into the category of **illegal drugs**, some of which have no medical value. These often have serious side effects, including death, and are usually addictive – in some cases, only one 'dose' is all that is needed for the body not to be able to do without it.

Social drugs such as alcohol and nicotine are legal (but age-controlled) and, despite the problems they can cause, are widely available and provide a huge amount of revenue for the government through taxation. However, as with all other drugs, social drugs can cause serious health problems and even death.

Objectives

Introduce the issues associated with drugs.

Identify religious teachings related to drug taking.

Key terms

Drug: a substance which, when taken, affects the body or mind.

Prescription drugs: drugs legally obtained only with a doctor's consent.

Drug abuse: using drugs in a way that harms the user.

Illegal drugs: drugs which are illegal to possess, sell or use, put into three classifications according to their potential harm and addictiveness.

Social drugs: legal drugs which are still addictive, such as alcohol, nicotine, caffeine, etc.

Activity

1 a Make a list of ten different drugs.
   b Categorise each drug as one of the following (some may fit into more than one category):
      ■ prescribed (legal) drugs
      ■ over-the-counter (legal) drugs
      ■ illegal drugs
      ■ social drugs.

Study tip

When answering a question on drugs, make sure that you write about the correct type of drug. If you are asked about illegal drugs, don't write about over-the-counter medicines or social drugs.

Religious beliefs about the body and mind

None of the six major religions permits followers to take illegal drugs. Some small groups within them may take certain drugs for a specified reason but the vast majority of believers think that taking such drugs is wrong because of the negative influence they have on the body and mind. A few Hindu holy men (sadhus) and a small group of warrior Sikhs called the Nihang use bhang, which is a mild form of cannabis obtained from the Indian hemp plant, but its use as an intoxicant is not allowed in mainstream Hinduism and Sikhism, which are strictly against illegal drug taking. Rastafarians and the Ethiopian Coptic Church – a small denomination of Christianity – allow cannabis to be used because it is a natural herb that God provided.

Jews, Christians (apart from the groups mentioned above) and Muslims are strongly against taking illegal drugs and the misuse of prescription drugs because of the damage they do to the body and mind that God created. Christians and Muslims compare the body to a temple created by God, the destruction of which is seen as a direct attack on God's authority. Buddhism is strictly against the use of illegal drugs because the fifth precept prohibits the taking of any intoxicating substance that can harm the mind.

A *Even prescription drugs can be fatal*

B *Prescription drugs can look like sweets*

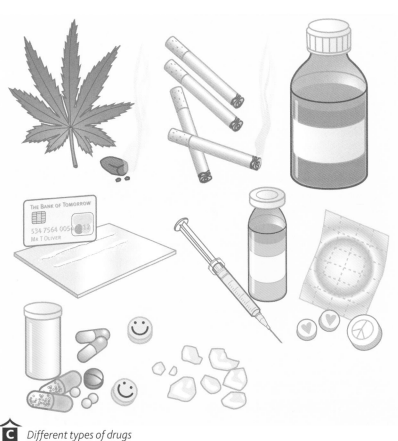

C *Different types of drugs*

Activity

2 'Religions allow medicines that affect the body, so they should allow drugs which affect the mind.' Write down your thoughts about this quotation and say whether you agree with it. Give your reasons.

Summary

You should now be able to identify the broad types of drug. You should also be able to discuss the issues associated with taking them and religious teachings relating to drug taking.

▇ Rights and responsibilities

We all have a right to medical care if we fall ill. In Britain, the National Health Service (NHS) ensures that this right is met in a way that everybody can access. We all have the right to a general practitioner (GP), or doctor, often attached to a health centre that provides other services for the well-being of its patients. If things go wrong and the GP is unable to provide the required treatment, he or she will refer a patient to someone who can help – usually at the nearest hospital or clinic. We have the right to drugs prescribed to help control or cure illness.

However, we also have the responsibility to ensure those drugs do not get into the wrong hands. There is a large illegal demand for prescription drugs such as anabolic steroids, which can be used as performance-enhancing drugs, and tranquillisers, such as temazepam. This demand is partly satisfied by some people illegally selling on prescribed drugs they no longer need or selling prescription drugs they have obtained from their GP by deception. Most GPs are not fooled, however!

Activity

1 **a** Imagine you have a friend who is selling prescribed drugs. What would you do about it? Explain your reasons.

b With a partner, prepare a conversation between yourself and this friend in which you try to advise them against selling the prescribed drugs.

There are other issues about the rights and responsibilities relating to the abuse of drugs. Some say they have a right to take whatever drug they like if they can afford to, but are not so forthright about their responsibilities to others when under the influence of drugs or addicted to them. Some may persist in the illegal selling of drugs, but shirk responsibility when drugs they sell cause death. In addition, their activities cost the public considerable amounts of money when they are sent to prison or want to be rehabilitated.

Objectives

Investigate rights and responsibilities associated with drugs.

Appreciate the legal status of different types of drug.

Discussion activity

With a partner, discuss whether we should have the right to take drugs if we want to, regardless of the responsibilities we have to other people.

Study tip

Remember you may be asked to put forward a point of view that you don't hold yourself. This is a skill you can learn.

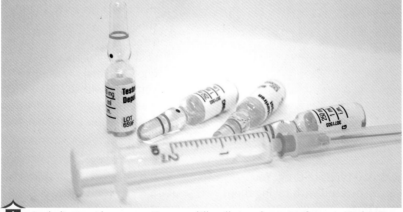

A Anabolic steroids are sometimes used illegally to enhance performance in sports

Drugs and the law

The legal status of different types of drug raises some interesting dilemmas.

- Social drugs such as alcohol and nicotine (in tobacco) are **legal**, despite the possibility of them causing a lot of harm to the user and others. Their sale is age-restricted to over-18s.
- Prescribed drugs are legal but only for the person for whom they are prescribed.
- Over-the-counter drugs are legal, although the quantity of some painkillers sold to any individual is restricted. Pharmacies can sell some over-the-counter drugs that non-specialist retailers (e.g. supermarkets) are not allowed to.
- Household **solvents** (e.g. glue, aerosols and gas lighter refills), which can be abused by sniffing, in some cases with fatal consequences, are not all legally controlled. Retailers are advised that it is illegal to sell them to people they believe may abuse them and some (e.g. gas lighter refills) are age-restricted to over-18s
- Illegal drugs are illegally manufactured and illegally sold (e.g. LSD, ecstasy and cocaine).

Caffeine is a mild stimulant that is not illegal, but can cause ill effects in some people. It is naturally found in coffee, tea, chocolate and soft drinks, and is used in some headache pills. It can also be taken in tablet form by people who need it to keep them awake or alert or to give them a temporary feeling of well-being. It is the most widely used mood-altering drug in the world. In large quantities it can be addictive and cause interruption of sleep patterns, problems with digestion and anxiety disorder leading to panic attacks. Regular users of caffeine can suffer withdrawal effects if they reduce or stop their intake. This can lead to headaches, fatigue, difficulty in concentrating, irritability, anxiety and depression. Yet caffeine is legal, not controlled in any way and regularly given to very small children in the form of chocolate and soft drinks.

B *Coffee and chocolate – two of the main sources of caffeine*

Key terms

Legal drugs: drugs that can be purchased legally. Some have age restrictions.

Solvents: some aerosols, glue and gas lighter refills abused by sniffing, which can cause hallucinations and can be fatal.

Caffeine: a mild legal stimulant found in coffee, chocolate, etc.

⚭ links

See pages 58–59 for the classification of illegal drugs.

Beliefs and teachings

Don't you know that you yourselves are God's temple and that God's Spirit lives in you? If anyone destroys God's temple, God will destroy him.

1 Corinthians 3:16–17

Activity

2 a Should the sale of caffeine be controlled? What do you think?

b Explain some of the problems that would be caused if the government were to control the sale and use of caffeine.

Summary

You should now be able to discuss the rights and responsibilities associated with drugs, and what the law says about them.

Drug classification

Since the Misuse of Drugs Act 1971 became law, illegal drugs have been graded as class A, B or C. **Drug classification** is based on how harmful and addictive each particular drug is. Those that are most harmful and addictive are put in class A, with the least harmful and addictive in class C. By doing this, the government is able to impose far greater sentences for possessing or selling class A drugs than for class C drugs. In addition, people can be in no doubt about the harm they could be doing themselves if they decide to take class A drugs. Despite this, official estimates show that in England in 2006 over 330,000 people were regular users of opiates such as heroin and crack cocaine – both class A drugs.

Activity

1 Why are illegal drugs classified as class A, B and C? Think of other reasons in addition to those given in this chapter. You can discuss this with a partner before you start writing.

A *Cocaine is a class A drug – overdoses can be fatal*

Some examples of illegal drugs

The table on page 59, gives some examples of illegal drugs, their classification, effects and punishments.

Activities

2 Note down the three categories, some examples and the maximum penalties for each.

3 'Drug classification doesn't seem to be working.' What do you think? Explain your reasons.

Research activity

Find out more on **www.talktofrank.com**

Objectives

Identify the three categories of illegal drug.

Understand why these categories exist.

Key terms

Drug classification: three legal categories by which illegal drugs are classified in British law according to the level of harm they do and how addictive they are.

Beliefs and teachings

Everyone must submit himself to the governing authorities, for there is no authority except that which God has established. The authorities that exist have been established by God.

Romans 13:1

Extension activity

'All illegal drugs should be Class A with Class A punishments.' What do you think? Explain your opinion.

Study tip

Try to give a specific example if writing about different classes of drug.

links

For more detail on the classification of cannabis, see pages 60–61.

Classification	Examples	Effects / Dangers	Legal punishment
A	Heroin ('smack')	A painkiller derived from the opium poppy. Snorted, smoked or injected, it gives an initial feeling of well-being. Overdose can induce coma and death. Very addictive.	Maximum 7 years in prison for possession; maximum life in prison for supply.
A	Ecstasy ('E')	Usually a white tablet, it is a stimulant often taken at parties and nightclubs. It can give a brief sense of euphoria followed by calm. Sweating and heart rate increase, and this can lead to fatal dehydration and kidney or liver problems.	As heroin
A	LSD ('acid')	An hallucinogenic drug which affects the mind. 'Trips' can last 8–12 hours, are unpredictable and cannot be stopped. It can cause depression, anxiety and death through accidents whilst under the influence.	As heroin
A	Cocaine ('coke', 'Charlie')	A white powder that is snorted or injected. It is a powerful stimulant with effects lasting about 30 minutes. After-effects can be depression, confusion and restlessness. It can cause heart problems and damage the inside of the nose. Overdoses can be fatal.	As heroin
A	Crack cocaine ('rocks')	Cocaine adapted to be taken by smoking. Similar effects to cocaine but more intense. Very addictive, and heavy use can cause fatal heart problems and convulsions. It also damages the lungs and causes chest pains. Overdose can be fatal.	As heroin
B	Amphetamines ('speed')	These stimulants increase wakefulness and suppress the appetite. They can cause depression and paranoia, increased heart rate and blood pressure in the short term and possible long-term heart defects and schizophrenia.	Maximum 5 years in prison for possession; maximum 14 years in prison for supply.
B	Cannabis ('pot', 'weed', 'skunk')	Comes from the marijuana plant as dried leaves or resin and is usually rolled with tobacco and smoked. It helps people to relax and heightens the senses, but can cause lack of motivation and long-term psychological problems including schizophrenia. Some varieties (e.g. skunk) are more powerful than others. It has a medicinal use for conditions such as multiple sclerosis, although it cannot be legally prescribed.	As amphetamines
C	Anabolic steroids	These are legal if prescribed by a doctor for a recognised medical condition, but they are often used by bodybuilders because they increase muscle bulk. They are outlawed by all sports and lead to lengthy bans. They can cause aggression, heart and liver conditions and various hormonal imbalances (e.g. breast growth in men, menstrual disturbance in women).	Possession is legal; maximum 14 years (previously 5 years) in prison for illegal supply.
C	Tranquillisers, e.g. temazepam	These are prescribed by doctors as a short-term treatment for anxiety or depression. They have a calming effect. Reactions are slowed, which increases the risk of accidents, and they are dangerous when taken to excess or with alcohol. They are illegal if supplied or used without a doctor's prescription.	Maximum 2 years in prison for possession without a prescription; maximum 14 years (previously 5 years) in prison for supply.

Summary

You should now be able to identify the three categories of illegal drug and specific examples within each category. You should also have an understanding of why the categories exist.

Cannabis

Cannabis is currently a class B drug. That, however, tells only a part of the story. It was graded as class B by the Misuse of Drugs Act 1971. However, since that date, cannabis use has increased, with few apparent ill effects. Users and campaigners for downgrading its classification point out that using alcohol and tobacco seem to have much worse effects on users' health and on society as a whole, despite the fact they can be used legally (subject to age restrictions). In addition, there is conflicting evidence about whether or not cannabis is harmful to health or addictive.

In response to these arguments, the government reclassified cannabis as a class C drug in 2004 and acknowledged that adults in possession of cannabis were unlikely to be arrested for possession. However, repeat offending or smoking cannabis in public or in the vicinity of children would result in arrest, caution or prosecution, and the drug would be confiscated. For young people, implementation of the law was different. They would be arrested if found in possession of cannabis, and reprimanded or charged in a police station. Referral to a Youth Offending Team for rehabilitation to prevent future offending was compulsory for a repeated offence. Dealing in cannabis still carried a maximum 14-year jail sentence or an unlimited fine, or both.

But in 2008 the government announced that, from early 2009, cannabis would revert to being a class B drug. The main reason for this is that since 2002 skunk cannabis – a much stronger form – has gone from having a 30% share of the market to an 81% share. This has increased the likelihood of users experiencing the long-term effects of the regular use of cannabis, which makes it more harmful and arguably more addictive.

Objectives

Look more closely at the legal position of cannabis.

Debate the reclassification of cannabis.

Key terms

Cannabis: a class B drug which is usually smoked, which some wish to be legalised.

∞links

For more discussion on the use of alcohol and tobacco, see pages 62–67.

A *Cannabis is now available in much stronger form – a reason for its reclassification*

In April 2008, Prime Minister Gordon Brown said:

> 66 *Given the changing nature of the stock of cannabis that is coming into our country and the greater damage that that appears to be doing to people who use it, there is a stronger case for sending out a signal that cannabis is not only illegal but it is unacceptable.* 99
>
> Daily Telegraph, *2 April 2008*

B   *Should cannabis be legal?*

Research carried out on the effects of cannabis has shown that:

- nearly 1,000 people a year now develop a long-term psychotic illness due to cannabis use
- mental health hospital admissions due to the effects of cannabis rose by 63% between 2002 and 2007
- in Britain, 500 people a week need medical treatment after using cannabis
- in 2007, there were around 150,000 people claiming disability living allowance (up from 63,000 in 1997) for conditions directly related to cannabis use.

It was also pointed out that the average age of a first-time user of skunk is 13, which raises fears about users' future mental health. Cannabis can be regarded as a 'gateway' drug, introducing users to dealers as potential future customers and raising the possibility of starting a habit that could develop into a life of addiction to class A drugs.

Activity

1 a   Write a speech of at least 250 words EITHER trying to persuade an audience that cannabis should stay at class B OR that it should go back to being a class C drug. Your partner should argue the opposite case to yours.

   b   Read your speech to your partner and allow them to question you. They should then read their speech to you and answer your questions.

Extension activity

Do you think cannabis is a 'gateway' drug? Give reasons to support your answer.

Study tip

In the examination, take care when arguing that cannabis should be made legal because it relieves pain in some conditions such as multiple sclerosis and cancer. Although this is a valid argument, it is a weak one because the number of people involved is small and so the argument does not affect the majority of people.

Summary

You should now be able to discuss the classification of cannabis and understand different arguments relating to its use.

3.5 Social drugs

The status of social drugs

Many supporters of the declassification of cannabis point to the existence of other drugs that cause more harm and addiction than cannabis, which are completely legal. Not only are they legal but, until recent policy changes related to advertising, they were portrayed as being glamorous.

Nicotine (as found in **tobacco**) and **alcohol** are classed as social drugs, which means they are legal, although a licence is required to sell them and their sale is restricted to people over the age of 18. However:

- This doesn't stop young people getting hold of tobacco and alcohol.
- Tobacco causes lung cancer, bronchitis and heart disease and other conditions.
- Over 120,000 people die in Britain each year as a result of smoking-related diseases.
- From 1 July 2007, it has been illegal to smoke in an enclosed public place or workplace.
- Both nicotine and alcohol can harm an unborn child.
- Alcohol is a depressant.
- Alcohol is involved in over 30,000 deaths in Britain each year, some caused by driving under the influence of alcohol.
- Alcohol causes liver damage, obesity and damage to the heart.
- Both nicotine and alcohol are addictive (nicotine more so than alcohol).
- Excessive alcohol can lead to antisocial behaviour including violence, vandalism and rape.

Objectives

Understand why people use social drugs.

Consider the consequences of taking social drugs.

Reflect on how money raised from taxation of social drugs is spent.

Key terms

Tobacco: used in cigarettes and cigars, it contains nicotine an addictive social drug.

Alcohol: an addictive social drug found in beer, wine, spirits, etc.

links

Look back at pages 60–61 to read about the reclassification of cannabis.

links

To remind yourself of the drug classification system, see pages 58-59.

Research activity

Create a short questionnaire to find out why people smoke and/or drink alcohol. Ask people across a wide age range to complete it. Ask only people you know.

A *Cigarettes and alcohol are addictive social drugs*

Activity

1   Make a list of reasons why you think people smoke, and rank them with the strongest reason first and the weakest last. Give reasons for your first and last choices.

Discussion activity

1   a   With a partner, discuss whether tobacco and alcohol should be made illegal and subject to a classification.

b   Write down the conclusions you reach and the reasons for them.

■ Taxes on tobacco and alcohol

Both smoking tobacco and drinking alcohol are expensive habits. Cigarettes are very heavily taxed in order to encourage people not to smoke (tax and duty account for around 80% of the cost of a packet of cigarettes). Alcohol is not taxed quite so heavily, but tax still makes up a significant amount of the cost in the hope that people will drink less. Heavy smokers and drinkers have to find thousands of pounds a year to buy their tobacco and alcohol. If the price rises, they have to either cut down (if they can) or find the money from elsewhere. This could of course leave a family with even less to buy the necessities of life.

Some of the money collected in tax and duty goes towards funding the National Health Service, which has to cope with the extra demands put on it by smokers and drinkers. In 2007, health problems caused by alcohol cost the NHS around £2.7 billion; smoking-related illness cost less. In the same year, the cost to the NHS of drugs to help people quit taking drugs, drinking alcohol and smoking tobacco was around £111 million. However, the tax and duty raised from the sale of alcohol was around £8 billion, with a similar amount collected from tobacco sales. So the total cost to the NHS was around 30% of the total revenue. It could be said that smokers and drinkers subsidise other areas of public spending (including education).

> **Beliefs and teachings**
>
> Make not your own hands contribute to your destruction.
>
> *Qur'an 2:195*

> **Study tip**
>
> You need to know reasons why some people smoke and/or drink, as well as why others prefer not to.

Activities

2   a   Study the figures in the above paragraph. Do you think smokers and drinkers subsidise other areas of public spending? Explain your reasons.

b   Should tax and duty on alcohol and tobacco be further increased? Explain why you think so.

3   What do you think would happen if everybody stopped smoking and drinking alcohol? Think of both positive and negative outcomes.

Summary

You should now be able to discuss the issues associated with social drugs and why people use them. You should also be aware of how money raised in taxation on social drugs is spent.

3.6   Why do people use drugs?

Why do people drink, smoke or use illegal drugs?

The question 'Why do people use drugs?' cannot be answered by considering alcohol, tobacco and illegal drugs together. Whilst reasons for drinking alcohol and smoking are similar in some respects, there are greater differences when illegal drugs are considered.

Activity

1 Spend 10 minutes thinking about why people drink alcohol, smoke tobacco and take illegal drugs. Write your list down. If you have time, compare your lists with your partner's.

Why do people drink alcohol?

People have different ideas about why they drink alcohol. Here is a selection of 10 reasons:

- They enjoy the taste of some alcoholic drinks.
- Pubs and nightclubs are good places to meet socially and drinking alcohol is part of that scene.
- They enjoy being under the influence of alcohol.
- They are addicted to alcohol.
- Their friends drink, so they want to.
- Family life encourages drinking alcohol at meal times.
- Alcohol is connected with celebrating success or special events.
- They think alcohol makes them more of a person and it gives them confidence.
- They are influenced by peer pressure.
- They are influenced by advertising.

A *Is it worth losing your concentration?*

Beliefs and teachings

Wine is a mocker and beer a brawler; whoever is led astray by them is not wise.

Proverbs 20:1

Why do people smoke tobacco?

Here is a selection of 10 reasons why people might want to smoke tobacco. Some are similar to the reasons for drinking alcohol:

- They enjoy the taste and sensation of smoking.
- They need to smoke to relax.
- They are addicted to nicotine.
- Their friends smoke.
- They have grown up in a smoking household so it seems like the normal thing to do.

Beliefs and teachings

There are four sins that are particularly serious (one of which is) ... using tobacco ...

Rahit Maryada

- They think smoking helps to keep their weight down.
- They think it makes them more of a person.
- They think it will not cause them harm even though it harms others.
- They are following role models who smoke.
- They think they will look antisocial if they refuse a cigarette when offered.

Why do people take illegal drugs?

Perhaps surprisingly, there are also at least 10 reasons why some people take illegal drugs:

- They are addicted to them (e.g. heroin, LSD, crack cocaine).
- Taking illegal drugs helps them to enjoy a night out (e.g. ecstasy, cocaine).
- They have progressed from legal drugs such as alcohol.
- They were tricked into taking illegal drugs.
- They are influenced by peer pressure.
- They are following role models in the entertainment business.
- Taking illegal drugs seems to improve poor self-esteem.
- They start to take them to help them cope with a crisis in their life.
- They mix with people who take and deal in illegal drugs.
- They are influenced by the way some media represent youth culture.

B *Is it worth risking your health?*

> ### Beliefs and teachings
>
> He must not get wilfully addicted to any ... substance of self-gratification; he must try to overcome such dependence through will power.
>
> *Laws of Manu*

Activity

2 a Add to the list you made in Activity 1 any reasons you didn't include.

  b Decide which you think are:

   i the top three reasons why people drink alcohol

   ii the three weakest reasons why people smoke tobacco

   iii the three reasons why people take illegal drugs that are the most difficult to overcome.

  c Compare your reasons with those of others.

  d Be prepared to explain to the class why you have selected them.

C *Is it worth endangering your life?*

Extension activity

1 a What is the strongest reason for not using alcohol, tobacco or illegal drugs? Discuss your ideas with a partner before you write anything down.

  b Is that a stronger reason than any of the reasons why people do use alcohol, tobacco and illegal drugs? Explain why you think so.

Study tip

If asked in the examination to give reasons, for taking illegal drugs, do not use bullet points but explain carefully each reason you give.

Summary

You should now be able to discuss the many reasons why people take drugs, despite strong reasons why they shouldn't.

3.7 Reasons for not using alcohol and tobacco

What does religion say about alcohol and tobacco?

For Sikhs, obedience to the kurahits rules out the use of alcohol and tobacco because they are intoxicants and because alcohol affects the mind and distracts it from God. Buddhism also does not allow the use of alcohol or tobacco because of the potential harm to the user and others. Both Buddhism and Hinduism teach that these substances create bad karma. However, although smoking is banned in public places in India, Hinduism allows drinking alcohol and smoking tobacco, as long as users do not become dependent.

In Islam alcohol is completely haram (forbidden) because it makes the mind unfit to concentrate on Allah and the duties involved in being a Muslim. Many Muslims do not smoke because they do not want to harm the body Allah gave them, but smoking, although discouraged, is forbidden only during the Ramadan fast.

Judaism and most of the Christian Church (exceptions being, for example, Methodists and the Salvation Army) do not forbid the drinking of alcohol in moderation. Most Christians use alcoholic wine in Holy Communion and Jews are encouraged to drink more than usual at Purim. Smoking is discouraged by both religions for the harm it does, though it is left to individual choice. Many Christians would believe it was harming the body God had created.

Objectives

Investigate religious attitudes to drinking alcohol and smoking tobacco.

Establish reasons why people might decide not to drink alcohol or smoke tobacco.

I'M JUST OUT FOR A GOOD TIME!

 A *A good night out?*

Beliefs and teachings

It is better not to eat meat or drink wine or to do anything else that will cause your brother to fall.

Romans 14:21

Beliefs and teachings

The mind of a drunken person becomes confused, then the confused mind commits sins ... a wise person should never even try wine and other intoxicants.

Arthashaastra of Kautilya

Beliefs and teachings

Concerning wine and gambling ... in them is great sin ... the sin is greater than the profit.

Qur'an 2:219

Beliefs and teachings

Drinking the wine, his intelligence departs, and madness enters his mind.

Guru Granth Sahib 554

■ Personal choices, public effects

It is likely that only a small minority of people in Britain, apart from Muslims, Buddhists and Sikhs (around 2 million people), would try very hard to persuade others that drinking alcohol is wrong, unless taken to excess. But some people are teetotal, a personal choice based on religious or social principles to do with the effect of alcohol on the body or on their own experience or that of friends and family. Most others drink alcohol for social reasons and for enjoyment or relaxation. A wine connoisseur would say that a glass of wine with a meal and a brandy after it enhances the enjoyment of the food.

∞links

Look back at pages 64–65 to read about some of the reasons why people do drink alcohol and smoke tobacco.

Activity

Do you agree that people should be allowed to drink alcohol and smoke tobacco if they wish? Give reasons for your opinion. You may want to deal with alcohol and tobacco separately.

B *Since 2007 smoking in indoor public places has been banned across the UK*

There may be more people who would try to convince a smoker that they shouldn't smoke, though. After all, every packet of cigarettes sold in Britain has a government health warning aimed at encouraging smokers to quit. Smoking is now widely understood to be bad for people's health and to cause disease and illness and is seen by many to be an antisocial activity. Nicotine replacement products, designed to help people stop, are also widely available and often free if prescribed by a doctor. Unlike those who drink alcohol or use illegal drugs, smokers can directly affect the health of those around them, the non-smokers, which is why Britain (along with much of Europe) has banned smoking in public places. However, smoking remains legal and, outside age restrictions, people are free to buy tobacco products and smoke them if they want. They would probably claim that the smoking experience relieves stress and gives them pleasure, and so they should be entitled to smoke.

Summary

You should now be able to discuss the different reasons, including religious ones, why people might or might not choose to drink alcohol or smoke tobacco.

A personal freedom?

> *It's my life and I'll do what I want with it* 99

> *It gives me the buzz I need* 99

> *But it's natural so it must be OK* 99

> *We are all free to do what we want* 99

Whilst there may be some debate over using alcohol and tobacco, there is less room for discussion of whether or not illegal drugs should be taken. Apart perhaps from cannabis, it is hard to think of any good reason, apart from personal freedom to do what you want, that would justify taking substances that are so addictive and so physically and mentally harmful. The short-term buzz that ecstasy and cocaine provide has to be weighed up against the negative effects on health, personal finances and the lives of others. Does the fact that opium is obtained from a natural source (the seeds of a particular species of poppy) mean it can be taken in the form of heroin? Rastafarians use that logic to justify smoking cannabis, but would definitely say 'no' to opium or heroin.

Discussion activity

1. a With a partner, plan a conversation between two friends going to a party. One has some cocaine and intends using it. The other is strongly against taking illegal drugs.

   b Later, the person with the cocaine is arrested for possession of a 'controlled substance'. They ask their friend for help. If you were this friend, what would you do? Why?

The supply of illegal drugs

The maximum penalties for supplying illegal drugs range from 14 years in prison for supplying classes B and C to life in prison for supplying class A drugs. However, in practice, sentences rarely reach the maximum. Some dealers are given a large fine and their supply of illegal drugs is confiscated, especially for first offences or supplying small amounts of lower-class drugs. In practice, the dealer on the street is often overlooked in a quest to find out who supplies *them*. It is estimated that between 60% and 80% of illegal drugs would need to be taken off the street for major drug traffickers to be put out of business.

Objectives

Investigate how taking illegal drugs affects other people.

Analyse problems associated with obtaining drugs.

Investigate religious attitudes to the use of illegal drugs.

Study tip

You could use any of these ideas to explain why some people take illegal drugs.

∞links

Look back at pages 64–65 to read about some of the reasons why people do take illegal drugs.

Extension activity

Do you think medical conditions caused by drug abuse should be treated free by the NHS, as at present, or should the person have to pay for treatment? Explain your reasons.

Discussion activity

2   Do you think individual street drug dealers should be punished more harshly? Explain your reasons.

In practice, taking illegal drugs out of supply can create further problems for society. If there is a shortage of illegal drugs on the street, maybe owing to a large amount being seized and confiscated, the price may rise, especially if the supply network has been hit by a seizure and needs to make more money to cover what has been confiscated. If prices rise, addicts have no choice but to find the extra money to feed their addiction.

Activity

1   a   How do you think an addict might find money to pay for their illegal drugs? Compare your answer with a partner's.

b   What problems do you think this may cause to them and others in society?

A   *A drug dealer*

The social consequences of illegal drugs

You have probably mentioned crime in your answer to the questions above. If an addict needs illegal drugs and has no money to buy them, the obvious remedy is to steal money or items that can be sold to raise the cash for drugs. Next day, nothing has changed and the cycle starts all over again. If the price of drugs rises (as is quite likely), the addict has to commit more crimes in order to be able to afford them.

In addition to the way they affect society, the addict will probably hurt those closest to them. If they still live with their family, their addiction is likely to dominate family life and cause hurt and upset to the very people who may be doing all they can to help. It is more likely, however, that an addict will live on the street or in a hostel, losing touch with their family who, even though they may have disowned them or even turned them out of the family home, will still care about their well-being.

What does religion say about illegal drugs?

Buddhism, Islam and Sikhism forbid the use of illegal drugs for the same reasons they forbid alcohol and tobacco. Christianity, Hinduism and Judaism also teach against the use of illegal drugs. For Christians, the emphasis is on the harm drugs do to the individual, the family and society. For Jews, such use is breaking the law, encourages a lack of self-control and causes harm. Christianity and Judaism teach that compassion and help should be given to addicts.

Beliefs and teachings

I will not take drugs or drink that confuse the mind.

Fifth Precept

∞ links

Look back at pages 66–67 to remind yourself of what religions say about alcohol and tobacco.

Summary

You should now be able to identify the ways illegal drugs are obtained. You should also be able to discuss the resulting social problems and religious attitudes to the taking of illegal drugs.

Research activity

Using the internet, find out more about what the religion(s) you are studying teach about illegal drugs. Find relevant quotations if you can.

Darren's story – a case study

Darren's early life

I'm 36 years old and come from a very loving family. But at the age of 14 I began to have problems at school. Exams stressed me, other pupils taunted me because I was overweight and I didn't have a girlfriend. I began to feel I didn't fit in, so to win acceptance I turned to stealing. I knew it was wrong, but it helped me to make friends and the girls began to like me.

I left school at 16 and began stealing cars. I even stole from my parents to pay for new clothes and alcohol. I constantly lied to them and told them I had started a new job, only to leave home at 8.00am to hang about the streets with my pals. Then I was introduced to cannabis and quickly became hooked. It seemed to boost my confidence. …

When I was 17, the police arrested me regularly and I spent a month in prison. Things got so bad that my parents kicked me out. At 19, I started doing speed at parties and at 20 I joined the rave scene and used ecstasy and acid tablets like they were sweets. By now I was selling cannabis to fund my habit. My run-ins with the police got worse and I spent another two months in prison. At 21 I started to use cocaine. I was at a rave and, having popped about four ecstasy pills, I thought, 'What the hell!'

In denial

… I had plenty of signs to tell me I was an addict but I was in denial. By the time I was 22 I started selling ecstasy and soon owed the dealers money.

I realised that if I didn't sort myself out I was going to get hurt. I tried methadone programmes, cold turkey, sleeping pills and short-term counselling, but all my efforts failed.

Within days of my girlfriend leaving me, I injected for the first time – not just heroin but crack as well. That was a near-fatal decision. … I was living from day to day by shoplifting. I smelled bad, looked awful and had no friends left apart from other addicts. All my veins collapsed in my arms, so I injected into my legs. They soon collapsed too and I switched to my groin. My weight plummeted to eight stone. I was in awful pain and lost my desire to live. I overdosed twice but was brought back by other addicts. The second time I actually wished they hadn't saved me. I was at death's door. I had a huge lump growing on my groin from the injections.

Finally at 28 I begged my parents for their help. They took me to hospital, where the abscess in my groin burst whilst I was in A&E. It smelled so bad. It was full of pus and blood. I was so lucky I was there

A *Drugs usually lead to a downward spiral*

because if that had happened on the street I would have died. I was kept in for a month and given methadone. I had three operations on my leg but it will never fully heal.

Rehabilitation in prison

Yet when I got out of hospital I still thought I could use heroin if I didn't inject! Soon afterwards I was picked up by the police yet again and this time got an 18-month prison sentence. Somehow prison worked out differently for me this time. Other addicts who were on the rehab wing of the prison urged me to join them and try getting clean. So I did. Then another inmate caught me using and I was thrown off the wing and back to 23-hour lock-up. But luckily my cell was adjacent to rehab and that same night someone called out, 'Darren, are you there?' It was the guy who split on me. He said, 'Darren, I told on you for your own good. We love you and want you to get clean. Don't give up.' Then about 15 to 20 grown men in prison were urging me to keep trying to get clean. It was the most powerful message ever and it gave me a new resolve to get back to rehab and kick my habit.

After serving nearly a year in prison I went straight to second-stage rehab and wasn't allowed out unless supervised. I knew that if I didn't do it I would suffer a relapse.

Fighting for recovery

To say my life has changed is an understatement. I haven't used illegal substances for nine years now.

But I'll admit it's not been easy. To start with, it was a struggle hour by hour. I had curbed my physical addiction but my psychological addiction involved a daily battle against my cravings. I kept a picture in my wallet of me at my lowest point, when my skin was yellow, my eyes were hollow and my body was skeletal. Whenever I had the slightest urge to use, I would look at that photograph. It was a reminder of what would happen if I succumbed.

Darren is now married with a young son and works as the Outreach Education Team Leader for **Drugsline**, visiting schools in south-east England.

> **Key terms**
>
> **Rehabilitation (rehab):** process by which addicts are helped to defeat their addiction to drugs.

> **Study tip**
>
> You won't be expected to write a case study in the examination, but you could refer to this one when writing about the harm illegal drugs do.

> **Activity**
>
> Choose from EITHER:
>
> 1 From what you have learned, write a fictional case study that shows how drugs can affect a person's life.
>
> OR
>
> 2 Write a letter from a member of Darren's family explaining how his addiction has affected them and how they feel about him.

> **Research activity**
>
> Find out more at www.drugsline.org

Summary

You should now be able to discuss the problems associated with drug addiction and its affect on other people.

What can be done about addiction?

Different attitudes to addiction

There are ways of helping people to beat their addiction. But some people think that addicts to drugs, alcohol or tobacco should be left to sort themselves out. They might ask why good money should be spent on people who have done nothing to deserve it.

Discussion activity

With a partner, work out a response to the attitude that addicts should help themselves rather than rely on others to help them. Use both religious and non-religious arguments.

Other people, whether religious or not, disagree with that attitude. They support efforts to help addicts through rehabilitation. Getting off illegal drugs without professional medical help is very difficult, but unless an addict has a lot of money to check into a private clinic (as some celebrities do), it can be difficult to obtain the help they need. Places on rehabilitation programmes are limited. Sometimes a prison sentence, which offers free rehabilitation, is the best way to kick the habit. However, not all prisons can provide such help and drug taking is often commonplace in them.

Despite some success stories, rehabilitation has a low long-term success rate. Many 'patients' make good progress whilst being treated and supported, but there is no real cure and constant effort is needed to resist temptation. Once 'clean', a patient may return to their previous environment, with the same risks and temptations, where drugs are easily available. Some do manage to change their lives and feel that their experience has given them the knowledge and understanding to help others.

A Celebrities can afford private rehabilitation clinics

Objectives

Know and understand ways of dealing with addiction.

Evaluate the effectiveness of rehabilitation.

∞ links

Look back at Darren's story pages 70–71 for ways that drug addicts might be helped.

Activity

1 a With a partner, discuss whether anything else can be done to solve the problem of illegal drugs.

b Of all the ideas, which do you think is most likely to succeed? Explain why you think so.

c Now consider which is least likely to succeed. Explain your reasons.

Is there a long-term solution to illegal drugs?

It is difficult to see an effective solution. Britain has a bigger illegal drug problem than any other country in Europe. The government spends around £1.5 billion per year on tackling the problem but no one is sure how effective this has been. For example, there are still 300,000 children growing up in homes where one or both of their parents are dependent on illegal drugs. So what can be done?

- More investment could be made in enforcement so that fewer illegal drugs reach the streets.
- Sentences on users and dealers could be increased.
- With more investment, rehabilitation could be provided and made compulsory for all addicts.
- More investment in improving life in socially deprived areas might reduce the number of young people starting to take drugs.
- Increased focus on drugs education in schools and the media may help.

Religious views on the importance of helping addicts

Whilst all religions condemn illegal drug taking, once a person has succumbed to the temptation of taking drugs and become addicted, believers are keen to help them conquer their addiction. For Sikhs, this is seen as sewa, the duty to help others in society. For Buddhists, it is part of 'right action' from the Eightfold Path, and shows metta (loving kindness) and karuna (compassion). Many Christians follow teachings such as 'It is not the healthy who need a doctor, but the sick' (Mark 2:17) and 'Whatever you did not do for one of the least of these, you did not do for me' (Matthew 25:45). These encourage them to help wherever they can. Hindus believe that ahimsa (no harming) and dharma (duty) help them to build good karma, although there is a belief that addiction is the result of previous karma. Whilst drug taking is condemned in Islam, followers are expected to help Muslims who succumb to the temptation of drugs. Judaism encourages assistance and counselling for addicts.

Study tip

Remember that, as well as teaching that taking illegal drugs is wrong, some religious people do try to help addicts.

Research activity

Find out about an organisation from the religion you are studying that helps addicts. Write a side of A4 about it.

Summary

You should now be able to discuss different ways of dealing with addicts and evaluate the effectiveness of rehabilitation.

Religious attitudes to drug abuse – summary

For the examination you should now be able to:

✔ understand the difference between prescription drugs, legal drugs and illegal drugs

✔ discuss religious beliefs about the body and mind

✔ understand the law relating to different types of drug and the classification of illegal drugs

✔ understand the legal classification of different drugs and discuss issues related to their use

✔ evaluate why people might smoke tobacco, drink alcohol or take illegal drugs

✔ evaluate the raising of taxes on social drugs and the use of those taxes

✔ discuss religious teaching relating to alcohol, tobacco and illegal drugs

✔ evaluate why some people might take illegal drugs and the effects on their own and others' lives

✔ evaluate the possible solutions to drug abuse

✔ discuss religious teaching relating to helping addicts

✔ discuss topics from different points of view, including religious ones.

Sample answer

1 Write an answer to the following exam question:
Explain how a religious person might help someone who is addicted to illegal drugs.

(4 marks)

2 Read the following sample answer.

> The best way of helping someone addicted to drugs is to shut them in a room so they can't get out. That way they won't get any drugs. If they go mad, so what – at least they won't take drugs again. Cruel to be kind.

3 With a partner, discuss the sample answer. Do you think that there are other things that the student could have included in the answer?

4 What mark would you give this answer out of 4? Look at the mark scheme in the Introduction on page 7 (AO1). What are the reasons for the mark you have given?

Practice questions

1 Look at the photograph below and answer the following questions.

(a) Explain briefly the meaning of the word 'drug'. *(2 marks)*

Study tip In order to explain, you must include some detail.

(b) Explain why some religious people might be against drinking alcohol. *(3 marks)*

Study tip Remember that it is important to think of reasons which religious people would use – this may involve a teaching of their religion.

(c) 'Religious believers should not smoke.' What do you think? Explain your opinion. *(3 marks)*

Study tip When you are asked this type of question, try to write about six lines.

(d) Give two reasons why religious people oppose illegal drugs. *(4 marks)*

Study tip When you are asked for two reasons, you must give two to gain full marks, including some extra detail to help you explain.

(e) 'Taking drugs should be a matter of individual choice and nothing to do with anybody else.' Do you agree? Give reasons and explain your answer, showing you have thought about more than one point of view. Refer to religious arguments in your answer. *(6 marks)*

Study tip Before you start writing your answer to the final question, think carefully of reasons why some people think taking drugs is a matter of individual choice and nothing to do with anyone else and reasons why some people have different views. If you have time, finish with a conclusion, without repeating yourself.

4.1 Crime and religious beliefs on law and order

The extent of crime

Over 30,000 **crimes** on average are committed in England and Wales each day, although the majority of these are not reported to the police. A crime survey estimated that there were 11 million crimes committed in England and Wales during 1981. The police received a report of fewer than three million of these. The difference between the two figures is called the 'dark figure' of crime. The British Crime Survey estimated that after 1981 the dark figure of crime increased until in 1995 it reached a peak of around 19 million. Now it has dropped back to less than 11 million. It is difficult to make exact comparisons with the past because the police recording methods have changed. However, it appears that crime incidents, although on average about twenty occur every minute, are not increasing. A report from the 2006 Offending, Crime and Justice Survey (OCJS) showed that most young people between the ages of 10 and 25 are law-abiding but around 6% were classified as frequent offenders (they had committed more than six crimes in twelve months). Do these figures show that there is something about human nature – perhaps greed or selfishness – that makes us all capable of wrongdoing and crime?

> **Discussion activity** 👥👥👥
>
> 1 With a partner, in a small group or as a whole class, discuss what the crime statistics show us about human nature.

Religious attitudes to crime

All the major religions recognise the importance of law and order in society. Without it there would be disorder and chaos. People would live in fear and be constantly worried about being the victim of criminal activities. Citizens have a moral duty to behave in a law-abiding manner or they deserve the punishment of the law.

Buddhists believe that if a person breaks the law his or her karma will be affected and the actions will have consequences. For Buddhists, this is not a case of God judging or punishing people, but a person's own karma will ensure that justice will eventually be done in either this life or the next.

Christians do not believe in karma but they have a similar teaching: 'A man reaps what he sows' (Galatians 6:7). Most Christians teach that criminals need to be punished but also forgiven and given a second chance (Luke 17:3–4). They believe that it is important to work towards stopping the causes of crime. Christians are encouraged to be law-abiding citizens.

Objectives

Examine the extent of crime in England and Wales.

Identify religious responses to the issue of law and order.

Key terms

Crime: an offence that is punishable by law, e.g. stealing.

A The Old Bailey, London

Beliefs and teachings

Hurt not others in ways that you yourself would find hurtful.

Udana-Varga 5.18

Beliefs and teachings

Make every effort to live in peace with all men and to be holy; without holiness no-one will see the Lord.

Hebrews 12:14

Hindus are encouraged not only to keep the laws that relate to general crime such as vandalism but also to fulfil their religious duties. Like Buddhists and Sikhs, they believe in karma and do not want the prospect of future suffering.

Muslims believe in the importance of law and order, and Shari'ah law is based upon four sources: the Qur'an, the Sunnah (practices of the Prophet Muhammad), the consensus of Islamic scholars and new case law, which has been decided by Shari'ah judges.

The idea of justice is clearly shown throughout the Jewish scriptures. The Torah emphasises the importance of the law and includes the Ten Commandments, which is central to the Jewish religion.

Beliefs and teachings

Follow justice and justice alone, so that you may live and possess the land the LORD your God is giving you.

Deuteronomy 16:20

But let justice roll on like a river, righteousness like a never-failing stream!

Amos 5:24

Sikhs recognise the importance of keeping the law. They believe that the consequence of criminal activity is the creation of bad karma and that it will result in the judgement of God.

Beliefs and teachings

Whoever vows to tyrannize over the humble and the meek,
The Supreme Lord burns him in flames.
The Creator dispenses perfect justice
And preserves His devotee.

Adi Granth, Gauri, M.5

B *The Ten Commandments*

Beliefs and teachings

Unrighteousness, practised in this world, does not at once produce its fruit; but, like a cow, advancing slowly, it cuts off the roots of him who committed it.

Laws of Manu 4.172

Beliefs and teachings

Allah doth command you … when ye judge between man and man, that ye judge with justice.

Qur'an 4:58

Study tip

Learn some quotations from the sacred writings in the religion(s) you are studying, which you can use in answering questions on crime and punishment.

Discussion activity

2　With a partner, in a small group or as a whole class, discuss why crime is a problem and why each of the major religions is concerned about it.

Activities

1　Explain why it is difficult to give accurate crime figures.

2　Explain religious beliefs about law and order.

3　'If you break the law you will always be punished in some way.' What do you think? Explain your opinion.

Summary

You should now be able to explain that crime is a considerable problem and you should know and understand the attitudes of religious believers to law and order.

The difference between right and wrong

It is important for society that people are brought up to understand the concept of what is right and what is wrong. Citizens have a **duty** and **responsibility** to be law-abiding or otherwise there would be chaos, as people would do exactly what they wanted without considering others. If parents and schools do not teach children the difference between right and wrong, and do not set a good example, young people will not respect others and may even get involved in crime.

Constantly seeing or being involved in unlawful activity blunts a person's **conscience**. Many religious believers teach that God has given each person an inner voice that informs them of the rightness or wrongness of an action before it is carried out. Planning or carrying out a wrong action creates a feeling of guilt. Non-believers argue that a conscience is a person's inner sense of what is morally right or wrong. Without being taught moral standards, the voice of conscience may not bother a person if they commit a crime.

Objectives

Investigate why people break the law and commit offences.

Key terms

Duty: a moral or legal obligation.

Responsibility: a duty to care for or having control over something or someone.

Conscience: the inner feeling you are doing right or wrong.

Case study

Stabbings

'Two teenage boys stabbed ... it's just another day of gang warfare in Peckham' was the headline news in the *Evening Standard* of 14 May 2008. Apparently, two 18-year-old boys were attacked with knives in separate incidents near each other on the same day. It was reported that the first attack took place in a fast-food restaurant when a gang of around ten youths wearing bandannas and sunglasses and wielding baseball bats pinned their victim down and stabbed him in the side. Around half an hour later two men jumped out of a car and stabbed the second victim in the chest.

Research activity

Use the internet or newspapers to find out what punishments have been given to those found guilty of stabbings or shootings. Use this information when doing the discussion activity on page 79.

What causes crime?

We frequently see sensational newspaper headlines of stabbings, shootings, muggings, vandalism and the like, but what causes people to do such things? Some possible reasons why people commit crime (although these are not excuses) include the following.

A *Feeling rejected and isolated*

Social reasons

Surveys show that the vast majority of young people who end up in prison have been excluded from school so they lack education and qualifications. Left without anything constructive to do, without money and positive parental guidance, they turn to crime. Lawbreaking may give them an adrenaline rush and a feeling of importance. Acquiring possessions makes them think that they have achieved something.

Abusive and violent parents and broken homes may provide poor role models and leave children ignorant of acceptable behaviour. Hanging around the streets and estates looking for something to do leads to boredom. Criminal activity offers excitement. Feeling isolated and rejected by people can also be a reason for someone deciding to get their own back on society.

Drug, gambling or alcohol addiction may be financed through shoplifting, burglary and prostitution or some other form of criminal activity.

B   *Addicted to drugs and alcohol*

Environmental reasons

During times of high unemployment, crime rates appear to rise. This may be partly because people who are out of work have financial problems and little to occupy their time.

Rivalry between gangs has led to people carrying knives and guns. Pressure to join such groups and retaliation against other gangs leads to more trouble.

Crime rates among those who suffer from inadequate housing, overcrowding and a deprived background are high. An uncared-for environment does not encourage responsible behaviour.

Psychological reasons

Criminologists say that the majority of people in prison are suffering from mental illness or psychological problems.

Some people say that human nature is naturally selfish and greedy and some will use any method to obtain wealth and power. They would argue that advertising encourages this approach.

Many criminologists believe that violence on television can influence people to try to copy it.

> **Study tip**
>
> It is important not only to know and understand the causes of crime but also to evaluate them and consider possible solutions.

> **Discussion activity**
>
> With a partner, in a small group or as a whole class, discuss what you think is the main reason why people decide to break the law. What should be done about it?

Activities

1   What is a conscience?

2   Explain the main causes of crime.

3   'Everyone knows right from wrong. All the so-called causes of crime are just excuses.' What do you think? Explain your opinion.

4   'Anyone found carrying a knife or gun should be sent to prison.' What do you think?

> **Summary**
>
> You should now be able to identify the reasons that are used to explain why some people become criminals.

Civil and criminal law

British law is divided into two categories – civil and criminal law. Civil law concerns disputes between private individuals or groups. Cases are taken to a small claims court or to the High Court if the matter is more serious. They include disputed wills, divorces and arguments between landlords and tenants. Criminal law is relevant when the state law has been broken. Cases involve the police gathering evidence and then forwarding it to the Crown Prosecution Service. Less serious cases are usually dealt with at a magistrates' court, where the decision about whether a person is innocent or guilty is made by three magistrates. More serious cases are heard in a Crown court, where, if a person pleads not guilty, 12 citizens are sworn in as the jury to listen to the evidence. A judge presides and passes sentence if the jury finds the defendant guilty.

Objectives

Identify the different types of crime.

Understand what is meant by a religious offence.

Types of crime

There are two kinds of offence. Non-indictable offences are less serious ones such as cycling without lights or driving at 36 mph in a 30 mph speed-limit zone. Offenders are not sent to prison for this type of offence. Indictable offences, such as rape or murder, are more serious. In this type of case, a person may face a prison sentence if found guilty.

Some offences fall into the category of **crime against the person**. The crime is directed against an individual or a group of people. This category includes serious crimes such as murder, assault and rape. It also includes slander, hate crime such as targeting someone for violent abuse, neglect of children and mugging. The British crime survey for 2006/7 said that 19% of crimes reported to the police were classified as violent offences. In almost half of violent crimes there were no injuries and only a small proportion involved serious violence such as murder.

The majority of offences are **crimes against property**. Crimes of dishonesty, such as burglary, vehicle theft, shoplifting, film and music piracy, account for nearly half the total number of offences. Property crimes also include criminal damage such as vandalism and arson.

Crimes against the state (a country) include terrorist activities, selling secrets to another nation (e.g. military documents), and false accounting in order to deceive the tax office so that less tax is demanded.

Four types of crime cover three-quarters of all recorded offences; these are car crime, burglary, violent crime and disorder (damage/antisocial behaviour).

A   *Speed limits should not be broken*

B *Burglary is usually punished by imprisonment*

Religious offences

Religious offences may or may not be classified as crimes. Religions have their own sets of laws and rules and breaking them would be seen by members of the faith as a religious offence or sin. For example, in the Christian and Jewish tradition, the Tenth Commandment says, 'You shall not covet your neighbour's house. You shall not covet your neighbour's wife, or his manservant or maidservant, his ox or donkey, or anything that belongs to your neighbour' (Exodus 20:17). Desiring something that belongs to another person is not a criminal offence, although believers would regard it as a sin, but the actual act of stealing from someone's house not only breaks the Eighth Commandment 'You shall not steal' (Exodus 20:15) but also the state law. Another religious offence is blasphemy, which is also illegal in some countries. Blasphemy includes insulting God or sacred things and the making of images of God. In some Islamic societies it is both a religious and a state offence to convert from Islam to another religion.

Discussion activity

With a partner, in a small group or as a whole class, discuss which type of crime you think is the most serious. Make notes on the opinions given, and the reasons for them.

Activities

1 Explain the difference between civil and criminal law.

2 Describe the different types of crime.

3 Explain what is meant by:
   a a sin
   b blasphemy.

4 'Religious offences are just as bad as breaking state law.' What do you think? Explain your opinion.

The aims of punishment

The aims of punishment

If a person is found guilty of a crime, the resulting penalty often addresses more than one aim of **punishment**. The main aims include the following.

Protection

The aim is the **protection** of potential victims from criminal activities. Sending a person to prison keeps them away from the opportunity of crime and so protects society. For example, murderers, rapists, paedophiles, drug dealers and terrorists may be locked away because of the danger they pose to the public. People are very fearful if these types of people are living in their community.

Retribution

Retribution is seen as 'getting even' with the person who has committed the crime. It is getting revenge and giving the criminal what they deserve. This may help the victim to overcome their resentment, as the perpetrator gets punished appropriately. An early form of retribution was based on *lex talionis* (the law of retaliation). This meant that the criminals should receive as punishment precisely those injuries and damages they had inflicted upon their victims. Most religious believers, however, take this to represent the idea that offenders should receive a punishment that fits the crime.

Deterrence

Some potential criminals may be put off committing a crime if they believe that they will be caught and dealt with seriously. The authorities hope that the prospect of harsh consequences will persuade those who would break the law to think again and decide that it is not sensible to commit the crime. Criminals who are caught are made an example of to persuade them and others not to live a life of crime. In many Muslim societies public beatings are used as **deterrence**. In some of the states in the USA, the death penalty is used as a warning to others not to commit murder. Roman Catholics used to use the prospect of excommunication (being excluded) from the Church as a deterrent for those who would potentially oppose its authority or teaching.

> ### Beliefs and teachings
>
> Eye for eye, tooth for tooth, hand for hand, foot for foot, burn for burn, wound for wound, bruise for bruise.
>
> *Exodus 21:24–25*

Objectives

Identify and understand the main aims of punishment.

Key terms

Punishment: something done to a person because they have broken a law.

Protection: keeping the public from being harmed, threatened or injured by criminals.

Retribution: an aim of punishment – to get your own back: 'an eye for an eye'.

Deterrence: an aim of punishment – to put people off committing crimes.

Reform: an aim of punishment – to change someone's behaviour for the better.

Vindication: an aim of punishment that means offenders must be punished to show that the law must be respected and is right.

Reparation: an aim of punishment designed to help an offender to put something back into society.

A *The police help to stop crime as well as catch criminals*

Reformation

People who have committed crimes may require help to understand that their behaviour is unacceptable and that they need to change their attitude and become responsible members of society (that is, to **reform**). Reformation means turning criminals into law-abiding citizens. It involves recognition that offenders need help to change their ways. For the criminal, the process might include repentance and a feeling of regret, which brings a determination not to return to criminal activities. Methods of helping to achieve this include offenders being required to attend group therapy sessions, in which their crimes are discussed and analysed, or meetings with their victims, or to work for the community (community service orders).

Vindication

Vindication is important because if people did not respect the law, then they would do exactly what they wanted and the result would be a breakdown of law and order. For example, if drivers took no notice of traffic lights, there would be chaos on the roads and many injuries and deaths would result. Laws are made to help people live in a way that will not damage the environment, other people and themselves, and citizens need to respect laws and not think that they can get away with disregarding them.

Reparation

The idea behind **reparation** and restorative justice is that the offender is asked to do something to make up for the crime they have committed. For example, a vandal may be asked to clean up an area of a town or village as a form of community service. Sometimes the punishment may take the form of fines or compensation payments, which help to make up for the trouble caused, for example by paying money to enable the victim to put the situation right.

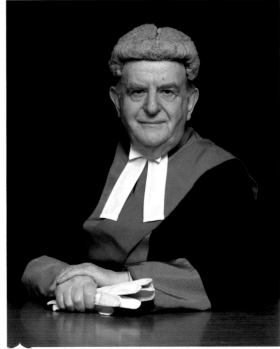

B Judges decide on cases brought to the Crown Court

⊂⊃links

To find out more about community service orders read pages 92–93.

⊂⊃links

To find out how religions respond to the aims of punishment, read pages 84–85.

Study tip

Make sure that you know the meaning of any technical terms for each of the aims of punishment included here. One of the short questions may ask you to define a specific aim.

Discussion activity

With a partner, in a small group or as a whole class, discuss the aims of punishment and put them in order of importance from 1 to 6 (1 being the most important). Give reasons for your decision.

Activities

1 Describe and explain the main aims of punishment.

2 'All punishment should be designed to get criminals to see the error of their ways.' What do you think? Explain your opinion.

3 'All criminals should be made to do unpaid work to pay back the community for what they have done wrong.' What do you think? Give reasons for your opinion.

Summary

You should now be able to describe and explain the different aims of punishment, giving examples of punishments that fit each one.

4.5 Religious responses to the aims of punishment

■ Religion and the aims of punishment

Buddhism

Buddhists believe that it is important to protect society from the actions of criminals but are not in favour of retribution. Getting revenge goes against the teaching of loving kindness (metta) and compassion (karuna). Using excessive cruelty to punish a criminal will injure both the offender's mind (making them bitter and resentful) and also the mind of the person doing the punishing. The best approach is to help the offender to have a change of heart and to modify/reform their behaviour. This would be in keeping with the Five Precepts. Reparation is also important because criminal activity creates bad karma and so making amends helps not only society but the lawbreaker as well.

Christianity

Most Christians do not support the idea of retribution but would support the other main aims of punishment. Christians believe that laws need to be upheld (the idea of vindication). They also believe in crime prevention and the need to work towards removing the causes of crime, which may include poverty, unemployment and bad social conditions. The most important aim of punishment is to reform criminals and to help them become law-abiding citizens. Most Christians believe that offenders should repent of their wrongdoing and receive both punishment *and forgiveness*, so that once the penalty is paid they have a second chance and can start afresh. Helping someone who has repented and is determined to change is a priority, and this is often achieved through reparation.

Hinduism

Hindus expect the law to protect people from criminal activities. In Hindu scriptures the king was expected to give suitable punishments to offenders (danda) with four main aims in view: deterrence, retribution, protection and reformation. Some of the suggested punishments were very severe but depended on the varna (caste) of the criminal. For example, the Brahmins were not allowed to receive corporal punishment. The threat of being relegated to a lower caste in either this life or the next was also a strong deterrent. Taking action to show they are sorry could make reparation and Hindus emphasise the need to reform or they will receive negative karma, which will affect them in the future.

Objectives

Understand religious responses to the aims of punishment.

∞ links

To remind you of the aims of punishment, refer to pages 82–83.

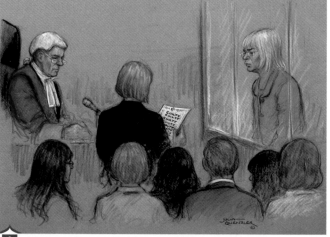

A Most people agree that laws need to be upheld

Beliefs and teachings

If your brother sins, rebuke him, and if he repents, forgive him.

Luke 17:3

Beliefs and teachings

In consequence of sinful acts committed with his body, a man becomes in the next birth an inanimate thing; in consequence of sins committed by speech, he becomes a bird or a beast; in consequence of mental sins he is reborn in a low caste.

Laws of Manu 12.9

Islam

Punishment in Islamic societies is designed to deter people from breaking the law. This is often achieved by public humiliation, such as a beating in full view of members of the local community. The aim is to ensure that the law is respected and to give the victims satisfaction. For example, adulterers can expect no mercy and a persistent thief who shows no sign of reforming may have a hand amputated as a warning to others. Muslims hope that offenders will repent, reform and seek forgiveness from Allah and their victims.

Judaism

Jews believe in the importance of punishment as a deterrent to those who would break the law. An important aim is for the offender to realise the wrong they have done and be determined to reform. This requires **repentance** and asking God's forgiveness. This is done through avoiding repeating the offence, giving money to charity and fasting. It is done especially on the Day of Atonement when Jews try to make amends for what they have done wrong by confession, prayer, repentance, fasting for 25 hours and donating to charity.

Sikhism

The concept of punishing for the sake of revenge (retribution) has no place in Sikhism. Punishment is given in an attitude of wishing to transform the offender so that they recognise their error and wish to reform. It is hoped that the lawbreaker will repent and so be forgiven by God. However, Sikhs recognise that some criminals are dangerous and society needs to be protected from them.

Beliefs and teachings

Do not turn around and strike those who strike you with their fists. Kiss their feet, and return to your own home.

Adi Granth 1378

Discussion activity

With a partner, in a small group or as a whole class, discuss the main similarities and differences between the different religions in their approaches to punishment.

Activities

1. Explain what the main aims of punishment should be according to the religion(s) you are studying.

2. 'Religious believers are too soft on criminals.' What do you think? Explain your opinion.

Summary

You should now be able to explain the attitudes of believers in the religion(s) you are studying towards the aims of punishment.

Beliefs and teachings

The woman and the man guilty of adultery or fornication, flog each one of them with a hundred stripes.

Qur'an 24:2

As to the thief, male or female, cut off their hands: a punishment by way of an example.

Qur'an 5:38

B *A Jew praying at the Western Wall in Jerusalem*

Beliefs and teachings

When justice is done, it brings joy to the righteous but terror to evildoers.

Proverbs 21:15

Key terms

Forgiveness: showing grace and mercy and pardoning someone for what they have done wrong.

Repentance: being truly sorry and trying to change one's behaviour so as not to do the same again.

Study tip

It is important that you understand and can evaluate the main aims of punishments for the religion(s) you are studying. Learn at least one quote from the sacred writings of the religion(s) you are studying and include it where relevant in answering the questions as it will help you obtain the higher level marks.

4.6　Young offenders and punishments

■ The age of responsibility

What should be done?

Pete is 12 years old and lives in an overcrowded two-bedroomed house with his three younger sisters and one brother. His dad is a heavy drinker and has been in and out of prison for the past 10 years. His mum is close to a nervous breakdown and Pete is left alone most of the time and has built up a lot of resentment. He has been excluded from school for a week for swearing at teachers and he is a difficult boy to control. With little to do he wanders around the housing estate very bored with life and he has already been in trouble with the police for vandalism, possessing cannabis and getting drunk. Some time ago he was given an ASBO (an Antisocial Behaviour Order) which requires him to be at home after 8pm but he frequently ignores this. Last night the police stopped him at 11pm and as this was the third time they had caught him breaking his order he will have to go to court.

Understand what the term 'young offender' means.

Consider how society should deal with young offenders.

Young offender: a person under 18 who has broken the law.

A　*Graffiti – youthful protest or a crime against society?*

Use the internet or library to find out more about ASBOs and ABCs (Acceptable Behaviour Contracts). Record how and why they are used.

This case study is made up, but many young people do find themselves in trouble with the law. If Pete was under the age of 10 it would be his parents who would be held responsible, as the age of criminal responsibility in England, Wales and Northern Ireland is 10. Until the age of 10 children are not deemed old enough to take total responsibility for their actions.

Some religions have ceremonies to mark the occasion when a person becomes an adult. In Judaism, parents are responsible for their child following Jewish law and traditions before the Bar Mitzvah, celebrated by boys at the age of 13, and Bat Mitzvah, celebrated by girls at the age of 12. They then become individuals to which 'the commandments apply'. In Britain a person is legally a minor until the age of 18, when they are given the full rights and responsibilities of adulthood.

■ Young offenders

In Britain, anyone under 18 who has broken the law is classified as a **young offender**. Minor offences are dealt with without going to court; for example, the police can use reprimands, final warnings, ASBOs or child safety orders. The aim is to prevent further offending and to give support at an early stage.

Young people committing more serious offences appear before a youth court. The youth court is a division of the Magistrate's Court and deals with people who are under 18 years of age. Any sentences are given by the young panel magistrates or district judges. If found guilty they may be fined or given a reparation order (e.g. they will have to repair damage they have caused), or receive a curfew order (they will need to be at home by a certain time). Serious cases are heard in a Crown court and the young person is held in custody. Those found guilty will not be sent to prison, but might be sent to one of three types of secure accommodation: secure training centre, secure children's home or young offender institution. Secure training centres are purpose-built centres for young offenders and they have a focus on education and rehabilitation. Secure children's homes are run by the local authority social services department and focus on attending to the physical, emotional and behavioural needs of the young people they accommodate. Young offender institutions are run by the Prison Service and accommodate 15 to 21-year-olds. Those under 18 are held in separate juvenile wings.

Britain has one of the highest rates of young people in custody in Europe and many people question the effectiveness of this sort of sentence, as young people are separated from their families. The Anglican Church recently called for an end to locking young people away but this was rejected by the Home Office.

B   *Should young people be locked away?*

Research activity

Use the internet to find out more about these three types of youth institution: secure training centres, secure children's homes and young offender institutions.

Activities

1   Explain the meaning of the term young offender.

2   Explain what is likely to happen if a young person commits a minor offence.

3   Give the three forms of secure accommodation that are used for young offenders who have committed serious offences. Explain the differences between them.

4   'Young people know right from wrong before they are 10, so the age of responsibility ought to be lowered.' What do you think? Explain your opinion.

5   'Young offenders should be given a beating rather than being locked away.' What do you think? Explain your opinion.

Discussion activity

As a class, discuss what you think should happen in Pete's case. You may wish to organise this as a court, with class members taking different roles.

Summary

You should now be able to explain how the law handles young offenders.

4.7 Prison

Prison

Britain's prisons are bursting with inmates. The prison population has almost doubled since 1993 – it is now over 80,000. Some prisons such as Kennet and Swansea have almost double the population that they were designed to serve. The steepest rises have been in the number of women and young people who are now locked up. The reason for this growth is not rising crimes rates or more convictions but the decision to send more people to prison for less-serious crimes and to give longer sentences. If this rate of increase continues, the prison population could soon exceed 100,000.

More people per head of the population are behind bars in Britain than anywhere else in Western Europe. This has put an enormous strain on the prison system as many of the prisons are over 100 years old and, although new prisons are being constructed, each new place costs approximately £100,000 to build. So many prisoners are forced to share a cell made for one, eating, sleeping and using the toilet in the same restricted space as another inmate for up to 23 hours each day.

The result, not surprisingly, is an increase in the reoffending rate from just over 50% at the beginning of the 1990s to nearly 70% now. Suicide rates in prisons are also rising as a result of desperation, overcrowding and long sentences.

Why send people to prison?

There are a number of reasons, which include:

- to protect society from dangerous and violent criminals
- to isolate those who deserve such punishment from their family and friends (retribution)
- to stop people reoffending, because they are locked away
- to act as a deterrent to others and ensure that the law is respected (vindication)
- to give offenders a chance to reflect on their actions and decide to reform.

The disadvantages of prison

Prison is an expensive option. It costs the taxpayer around £30,000 a year to keep someone in prison. There are also other problems with prisons, which include:

- they are often called 'schools for crime' – prisoners can educate each other in criminal methods
- prisons often breed resentment, bitterness and a determination to get back at society
- most prisoners reoffend on release, so the system does not bring about reform
- a prison record makes it very difficult to get a job on release, which may lead back into crime

A *Is prison the best place for all offenders?*

B *What are the disadvantages to locking people up?*

- offenders' families suffer through no fault of their own, e.g. children are deprived of a parent
- relationships often break down while a person is in prison.

Religious beliefs about prison

All the major religions accept the need for prisons. **Imprisonment** is seen as necessary to deprive offenders of their freedom and prevent them continuing a life of crime. Religions support the idea of seeking to reform offenders, so that on release they become responsible and law-abiding members of society. Therefore they support the idea of constructive work and education, so that inmates can learn worthwhile skills, and medical programmes to help prisoners overcome drug or alcohol addiction.

Christians have been actively involved in **prison reform**. In Britain, Buddhist, Muslim and Christian chaplains regularly visit inmates and also help prisoners' families. Christians may take their inspiration from the parable of the sheep and the goats (Matthew 25:31–46). Jewish rabbis and rabbinical students also visit and counsel prisoners and assist their families. Hindus encourage meditation and education as a means of helping prisoners to realise that they need to change. Sikhs have demanded reform because in some countries they have been forced to have their hair cut and have not been allowed to wear turbans.

Key terms

Imprisonment: when a person is put in jail for committing a crime.

Prison reform: a movement that tries to ensure offenders are treated humanely in prison.

∞ links

You will find more about prison reform on pages 94–95.

Study tip

Make sure you know arguments for and against the effectiveness of prison in achieving the aims of punishment.

Beliefs and teachings

'When did we see you sick or in prison and go to visit you?' The King will reply, 'I tell you the truth, whatever you did for one of the least of these brothers of mine, you did for me.'

Matthew 25:39–40

Discussion activity

With a partner, in a small group or as a whole class, discuss the effects of prison and whether or not you think the UK prison system is an effective form of punishment.

Activities

1. Explain the advantages and disadvantages of the prison system as a form of punishment.

2. Explain religious attitudes to prisons.

3. 'Prisons should educate offenders and then they would not commit crimes.' What do you think? Explain your opinion.

Extension activity

Use the internet or library to find out more about conditions in Britain's prisons, including the extent of overcrowding, the need for modernisation and the efforts being made to encourage prisoners to reform.

Summary

You should now be able to explain some of the advantages and disadvantages of keeping someone in prison and what religions believe about prison as a punishment.

4.8 Capital punishment

Capital punishment in the UK

In 1965 the UK Parliament voted to abolish the **death penalty** for a five-year experiment and in 1969 made the abolition permanent. All attempts to reinstate it have failed. Three people executed before the abolition have received posthumous pardons – Timothy Evans, Mahmood Mattan and Derek Bentley. There have been several cases since in which convicted murderers have been released because it was felt that the verdicts were unsafe, for example the 'Birmingham Six'.

Arguments for the death penalty

- Retribution – Terrorists and murderers deserve to die – 'a life for a life'.
- Deterrence – The death penalty deters people from doing horrendous crimes because they know if they are caught they will die.
- Protection – The public needs to be protected. However, those given a life sentence are often let out of prison after about 15 years.
- Finance – It costs taxpayers thousands of pounds to keep murderers alive in prison.

Arguments against the death penalty

- Mistakes – Innocent people have been executed.
- Protection – Putting a murderer in prison protects society.
- Deterrence – There is no evidence that the death penalty is more of a deterrent than life imprisonment.
- Reformation – Reformed criminals can be an enormous influence for good.
- Right – Only God has the right to end a person's life.

Religious beliefs about capital punishment

Buddhism

There is no single Buddhist policy on capital punishment. The death penalty is not in keeping with 'I undertake to abstain from taking life', the First Precept, and Buddhist teaching on non-violence and compassion. However, despite Buddhist teachings, some countries where Buddhism is the official religion do retain the death penalty as a deterrent, for example Bhutan and Thailand.

Christianity

Some Christians support capital punishment using the principle of 'Whoever sheds the blood of man, by man shall his blood be shed' (Genesis 9:6). They see the threat of the death penalty as a deterrent that helps to prevent serious crime. In America, many people, including Christians, support capital punishment for convicted murderers and the use of lethal injections or the electric chair.

A Murderers used to be hanged in Britain

B In the USA there are several thousand prisoners awaiting execution

Other Christians doubt whether capital punishment is a deterrent and oppose it because an innocent person might be executed and it removes the possibility of repentance. They believe that only God has the right to take away life (Acts 17:26).

Hinduism

There is a diversity of opinion in Hinduism regarding the death penalty. India retains capital punishment and this is supported by sacred writings. However, the teaching of ahimsa (non-violence) opposes taking life, violence and revenge.

Islam

Most Muslim countries retain the death penalty for murder. In some places it is also available if a Muslim converts to another religion or makes statements attacking Islam. The next of kin of the victim sometimes accepts financial compensation instead of the offender being executed.

> ### Beliefs and teachings
>
> O you who believe, retaliation is prescribed for you in the matter of the slain …
>
> *Qur'an 2:178*
>
> If anyone is killed unjustly, we have granted the right of retribution to his heir.
>
> *Qur'an 17:33*

Judaism

Israel has not abolished the death penalty, but the standard of proof is so strict that in practice capital punishment is not used. It exists primarily as a deterrent and not as retribution. The minimum requirement is two independent eyewitnesses, as circumstantial evidence is not enough. The Torah includes several offences that could incur the death sentence, but the only person to be executed since the formation of Israel was Nazi war criminal Adolf Eichmann in 1962.

Sikhism

The only time that Sikhs have had an independent nation was during the reign of Maharaja Ranjit Singh (1799–1839) in the Punjab, and capital punishment was not allowed. Sikhs believe that a civilised society should not descend to the level of murderers by taking revenge through the death penalty. There is always the possibility of executing an innocent person and such an error is irreversible.

> ### Activities
>
> 1 Explain the legal situation regarding capital punishment in Britain today.
>
> 2 'No one has the right to take life except God.' What do you think? Explain your opinion.

> ### Beliefs and teachings
>
> By killing an assassin the slayer incurs no guilt.
>
> *Manusmriti 8.351*
>
> An eye for an eye ends up making the whole world blind.
>
> *Gandhi*

> ### Study tip
>
> Be able to evaluate the arguments for and against capital punishment and use teachings from the religion(s) you have studied to support your points.

> ### Beliefs and teachings
>
> I take no pleasure in the death of the wicked, but rather that they turn from their ways and live.
>
> *Ezekiel 33:11*

> ### Discussion activity
>
> Organise a class debate to discuss whether or not Britain should have capital punishment.

> ### Summary
>
> You should now be able to explain religious beliefs about the death penalty and use reasons to explain why some people support it and others oppose it.

Community service

Offenders who have committed crimes for which they could be sent to prison for months rather than years may be given **community service** instead. Community service orders (CSOs) may be suitable for offences such as driving whilst disqualified, non-payment of fines or antisocial behaviour. The aim is to combine punishment with changing offenders' behaviour and making amends to the community.

Sentences range from 40–240 hours and involve compulsory supervised unpaid work, which is stipulated by the court. Projects include cleaning up the environment, reading to senior citizens, helping at a local library or charity shop, and gardening for the elderly or handicapped. Sometimes the offender is also given a curfew (a time from which they must remain at home until the next day) and forbidden to go to certain areas in their community. Occasionally, treatment for drug or alcohol abuse or mental health problems is also given to the offender.

Some see this as a soft option and the criminal may continue to break the law while doing the community service. Others regard it as much better than prison because it is far cheaper (less than a tenth of the cost), allows the offender to keep their day job, gives them less contact with other criminals and has been shown to have a much greater success rate in reforming the offender than prison.

A *Community service like litter picking can have noticeable benefits*

B *Gardening for the elderly is another form of community service*

Key terms

Community service: unpaid work that an offender performs for the benefit of the local community rather than going to prison.

Electronic tagging: an offender has to wear an electronic device which tracks their movement to ensure restrictions of movement are observed.

Fine: money paid as punishment for a crime or other offence.

Probation: an alternative to prison where an offender has to meet regularly with a probation officer to ensure that they do not re-offend. Movement may be restricted.

Electronic tagging

Prisoners serving between three months and four years can be released early provided they agree to a Home Detention Curfew Order. This ensures that they complete their sentence at home. Trials using **electronic tagging** took place in the late 1990s and the system is now used on a wider scale. Around 2,000 offenders are now fitted with electronic tags at any one time. This is a much cheaper option than prison, costing around £2,000 a year.

A monitoring unit in the home is connected to a central control room by a telephone line. As technology develops, more options are becoming available such as permitting a sex offender to leave home because the electronic tag will alert the authorities if the offender goes within a hundred metres of a school or park. So far, only 2% of offenders have committed more crimes while tagged and most of those have been driving offences.

Fines

Fines may be used by courts for a wide variety of offences. In a magistrates' court the maximum fine is £5,000, but there is no limit to the amount the court can fine. Fines reflect the seriousness of the offence and the offender's financial situation. Less-serious offences, such as parking tickets and speeding, have fixed penalty notices but those accused may contest the case in court.

Probation

Sometimes offenders are given suspended sentences, which means that if they get into trouble again within a specified time they will go to prison. Often the judge or magistrate may feel that, with help, the offender should be able to avoid breaking the law again. In these cases they may be given a **probation** order instead. The offender then has to report to a probation officer on a regular basis, for example once a week. The probation officer gives advice, helps the offender obey the law, and reports to the court about the progress being made. This type of punishment enables offenders to continue in their job, does not deprive them of their freedom, family and friends and, at the same time, gives support to help them reform.

C *The penalty for speeding is often a fine*

Discussion activity

With a partner, in a small group or as a whole class, discuss the value of these types of punishment.

Activities

1 Explain what is meant by community service orders, electronic tagging, fines and probation.

2 Explain the advantages and disadvantages of each type of punishment.

3 'CSOs, fines or electronic tags do not punish offenders enough.' What do you think? Explain your opinion.

Summary

You should now be able to explain how community service orders, electronic tagging, fines and probation may be used and the advantages of these punishments as alternatives to prison.

Parole

Having served the majority of their prison sentence, prisoners may be eligible to be considered for **parole**. If their sentence is less than 15 years, the parole board decides on the application. Serious criminals, who have been sentenced to over 15 years, have their cases reviewed by the Home Secretary. Whether or not an application is successful depends on a number of factors, such as behaviour while in prison, the nature of the offence, home circumstances and their plans on release.

If successful, they are released before they have served the full sentence, but they will need to report to a parole officer on a regular basis. If the request for parole is refused the prisoner may apply again after 12 months. If the conditions of parole are broken, the offender may be returned to prison.

Life imprisonment

Life imprisonment is the most severe punishment that can be given in Britain, but this does not necessarily mean that the prisoner will spend the rest of their life locked away. In some cases the offender will die in prison, as happened with Myra Hindley and Harold Shipman, but currently there are fewer than 50 prisoners who have been given a sentence that means they will remain in prison for the rest of their life.

The average life sentence is about 15 years before the criminal becomes eligible for parole. The trial judge can set a much longer term than this if the offence is a particular grave one. The prospect of release does give hope to prisoners, as the imposition of a long sentence can have a bad psychological impact. However, victims and their relatives might not be so happy at the thought that a convicted murderer, for example, might be allowed out of prison one day.

Objectives

Understand what is meant by parole, life imprisonment and early release.

Consider issues concerning prison reform.

Key terms

Parole: when a prisoner is released without having completed their sentence, because they have behaved well and accepted their guilt. The prisoner is monitored to try to ensure that they do not re-offend.

Life imprisonment: a prison sentence that (theoretically) keeps people in prison until they die.

Early release: when a prisoner is allowed out of prison even though they have not completed their sentence, or fulfilled the criteria for getting parole.

A *Should life imprisonment mean a life behind bars?*

Early release

Sometimes a prisoner is given **early release** before they are eligible for parole. This may be due to a political decision to give early release to those regarded as a low risk to society in order to relieve overcrowding in the prison system. Sometimes a prisoner is released early because they have demonstrated good behaviour, repented and convinced the authorities that they have reformed. There are always risks – the victims of the original crime might feel such a decision is unfair and the person released might reoffend. However, early release does give the offender a second chance and an opportunity to become a law-abiding citizen.

Prison reform

Many people, including religious believers, think that prison reform is needed. Christianity has a history of campaigning for it. For example, Elizabeth Fry (1780–1845), a member of the Society of Friends (Quakers), was instrumental in getting conditions improved in Newgate women's prison. Also in Britain, organisations such as the Howard League for Penal Reform and the Prison Reform Trust are working now to improve conditions for prisoners. They are very concerned that overcrowded conditions do not help prisoners to reform and they think that prisons should be reserved for the worst offenders rather than used for people who have committed relatively minor offences, such as not paying fines, or those with mental problems. Currently there are around 5,000 people in prison waiting for transfer to psychiatric care. Other people disagree with giving prisoners better conditions because they say prisons will become just like holiday camps and will no longer be a deterrent to crime.

Other people are very concerned that most prisoners are reoffending when they are released instead of reforming. Hindus in India are encouraging education and meditation in prisons as a way of repairing the minds of lawbreakers.

The organisation Action for Prisoners' Families, as well as others, believes that more support should be given to the families of those in prison.

B   *Should a prisoner be given another chance?*

Study tip

Make sure you can use arguments for and against parole, early release and prison reform. These are topics which are very controversial and so are likely to be used in evaluation questions.

Research activity

Use the internet or library to find out more about Elizabeth Fry, the Howard League for Penal Reform, the Prison Reform Trust or Action for Prisoners' Families.

Activities

1   Explain how the system of parole and early release is used in Britain.

2   Explain the work of organisations that wish to reform prisons.

3   'Religious believers think that everyone deserves a second chance.' Do you agree? Explain your opinion.

Discussion activity

With a partner, in a small group or as a whole class, discuss the following statement: 'Prison conditions should be made harsher not easier and life imprisonment should really mean life.'

Summary

You should now be able to discuss what life imprisonment means and the issues concerning parole, early release and prison reform.

4

Religious attitudes to crime and punishment – summary

For the examination you should now be able to:

✔ explain religious beliefs about law and order

✔ explain the concepts of right and wrong, conscience, duty and responsibility

✔ describe and evaluate the causes of crime

✔ understand the different types of crime

✔ explain the aims of punishment

✔ evaluate whether or not the different forms of punishment achieve the aims of punishment, including consideration of young offenders, imprisonment, parole and early release and the death penalty

✔ evaluate alternatives to prison and issues concerning prison reform

✔ discuss topics from different points of view, including religious ones.

Sample answer

1 Write an answer to the following exam question:

'No one should ever break the law.'

Do you agree? Give reasons for your answer, showing that you have thought about more than one point of view. Refer to religious arguments in your answer.

(6 marks)

2 Read the following sample answer, which has some good points in it, and consider whether the student has focused fully on the statement:

> Religions teach people the difference between what is right and what is wrong. For example, Khalsa Sikhs follow the Rahit Maryada and wear the 5Ks and Jews follow the Ten Commandments. Believers should try not to break the law because they would suffer from a guilty conscience and they know that it is their duty and responsibility to be law-abiding citizens. Christians believe that God put the authorities

> in power to make rules and regulations to protect society (Romans 13).

> Sometimes, however, people break the law accidentally or in a minor way. Also, sometimes the law contradicts religious laws, for example, when Sikhs were told that they had to remove their turbans and wear crash helmets when riding a motorbike. This makes it difficult sometimes to keep the state law, so although I agree that religious believers should try not to break the law, it isn't always easy to do this.

3 With a partner, discuss the sample answer. Do you think that there are other things that the student could have included in the answer?

4 What mark would you give this answer out of 6? Look at the mark scheme in the Introduction on page 7 (AO2). What are the reasons for the mark you have given?

Practice questions

1   Look at the photograph below and answer the following questions.

(a) Explain, using an example, what is meant by a 'religious offence'.   *(2 marks)*

Study tip Make sure you give a full explanation of the phrase, including an example.

(b) Give **three** ways in which a young offender may be punished by the law.   *(3 marks)*

Study tip You will get one mark for each correct way you include, so remember to include three for top marks.

(c) 'Prisoners should be given religious teaching.' What do you think? Give reasons for your opinion.   *(3 marks)*

Study tip Remember that even if you are asked for your opinion, you will actually get marks for the reasons you give.

(d) Explain **two** of the aims of punishment.   *(4 marks)*

Study tip When a question asks you to explain two things, you will earn two marks for each explanation (provided they are correct). If you give only one, you can gain a maximum of only two marks.

(e) 'Greed and selfishness are the main causes of crime.' Do you agree? Give reasons and explain your answer, showing you have thought about more than one point of view. Refer to religious arguments in your answer.   *(6 marks)*

Study tip Remember, when you are asked if you agree with a statement you must show what you think and the reasons why other people might take a different view. If your answer is one-sided, you will achieve a maximum of only four marks. If you make no comment about religious belief or practice, you will achieve no more than three marks.

Religious attitudes to the rich and the poor in British society

5.1 Introduction to the rich and the poor

■ Who are the rich and the poor?

Our society includes very rich people and very poor people as well as the vast majority who fall between these two extremes. The rich have acquired or inherited **wealth** in the form of money, possessions and investments. They have more money than they need to provide the basic necessities of life such as food and a home. In addition, they are able to buy luxuries, holidays and cars, and have savings in the bank or other investments. Their lives are comfortable and they have few financial worries.

A Wealthy people can afford many luxuries that ordinary people cannot

B Poor people can only dream of luxury

On the other hand, anyone living in **poverty** struggles to afford food and the basic necessities for themselves and their family. Some will have a home, but it may be unsuitable for their purpose and they may be behind with their rental or mortgage payments. Others will be homeless, whether through difficult circumstances or because their own choices have led to that situation.

Although these summaries describe stereotypes, they will help you to understand a little about what it would be like to be very rich or very poor.

Objectives

Understand who the rich and the poor in society are.

Consider why society is so unequal.

Key terms

Wealth: a large amount of money or investments.

Poverty: being without money, food or other basic needs of life (being poor).

Debt: situation where a person or organisation owes more money than they possess.

Study tip

Make sure you understand and can explain what the terms 'rich' and 'poor', 'wealth' and 'poverty' mean.

Activity

1 a In your opinion, which of these items would a person classed as poor *not* be able to afford?

   home   television   computer   fridge   food   smart clothes   passport   cigarettes   alcohol   car   computer games console   pet   microwave

   b Rank these items in the order in which they are important in your life. Explain your positioning of the most and least important.

Extension activity

Spend a couple of minutes reflecting on what life would be like without some or all of the items in Activity 1. Write some bullet points to note some of the changes to lifestyle that would result from a lack of these items.

■ A few facts

Here are a few facts about different people's financial situations in Britain in 2008:

- The British bank Alliance & Leicester was taken over by the Spanish Santander Group. Four of Alliance & Leicester's top directors were offered a bonus amounting to 125% of their annual salary if they continued to work for the bank until December 2009. This works out at between £½ million and £¾ million each in addition to their normal salary of between £400,000 and £600,000 per year.

- Top Premiership footballers earn more than £5 million per year from their clubs.

- Currently, the average worker can expect to earn around £1 million before tax in their lifetime. Many will earn much less than this.

- The cost of buying the average house was a little less than £200,000.

- The minimum wage was £5.73 per hour, resulting in take-home pay of about £200 per week.

- Total personal **debt** (including mortgages, loans, credit cards, etc.) was estimated to be about £1.44 trillion.

Discussion activity

Discuss the facts above. For example, do you think it is fair that people can earn such different amounts? In pairs or as a group, what conclusions can you make?

■ Is equality possible?

Many people would prefer there to be less of a difference between the rich and the poor. But complete equality, where people have the same amount of wealth, is very likely to remain an ideal. Communist philosophy attempts to close the gap between rich and poor (and some religious teachings share this ideal), but other people think that complete equality is not desirable.

Activities

2 Think of the advantages and disadvantages of equality, where people have the same amount of wealth. Discuss this with a partner, if it would help.

3 'Total equality between people would cause more problems than it would solve.' Do you agree? Give reasons for your answer, showing you have thought about more than one point of view.

Summary

You should now be able to discuss who the rich and the poor in society are and why society is so unequal.

⬭ links

To find out more about the minimum wage, see page 109.

Research activity 🔍

Find out how much would need to be repaid over 25 years on a mortgage of £200,000 at current rates of interest.

Beliefs and teachings

Everything animate and inanimate that is within the universe is controlled and owned by the Lord. One should therefore accept only those things necessary for himself, which are set aside as his quota, and one must not accept other things, knowing well to Whom they belong.

Sri Isopanisad 10

⬭ links

Read about religious attitudes to equality on pages 100–101.

General principles

Most religions acknowledge that there will always be rich and poor people. Religious founders and leaders throughout the centuries have seen that this is the case, and religions recognise that it will go on being so. They do not teach that equality in respect of money and possessions is necessary. Buddhism, Hinduism and Sikhism, which believe in reincarnation or rebirth, teach that whether one lives in wealth or in poverty depends on one's previous life.

Instead, religions teach that a different type of equality is desirable – one in which each person is valued and shown equal care and respect. They also teach that it is how wealth is acquired and used that is important – whether a person got rich by exploiting others and whether their wealth leads to greed and selfishness.

Many people, religious or not, would object to people being exploited, especially to increase an individual's personal wealth. Such exploitation might involve paying workers below the minimum wage or charging high prices for products simply to increase profits. This type of behaviour increases the gap between rich and poor, and causes more hardship for the poor.

All religions teach that spiritual riches are more important than material riches. What matters is what a person does with their wealth, not how much wealth they have. Jesus said to his followers that no one knows the hour or day of their death and riches built up on earth cannot be taken into heaven.

Hinduism, Buddhism and Christianity value ascetics, monks and nuns, who give up personal wealth to devote their lives to their faith. Some orders withdraw from everyday life altogether, while others devote some of their time to helping the poor and disadvantaged in the community.

However, that is just one way of achieving a spiritual goal. All religions expect rich people to use their wealth to help others, for example by supporting charities that help the poor – which is something a monk cannot do. This responsible use of wealth is another way in which people can reach their spiritual goals.

What each religion teaches

Buddhism

The Buddha left a wealthy life for a poorer one because wealth can lead to craving (tanha) and selfishness, which cannot result in true happiness. Ascetics, monks and nuns are respected for giving up money and possessions. However, the Buddha's middle way lies between wealth and poverty, recognising that there are basic necessities that apply to everyone. Wealth must be earned honestly in a way that respects the Eightfold Path.

Objectives

Investigate religious attitudes to the rich and the poor.

Consider whether and how we should strive for equality.

links

To read more about the minimum wage in Britain, see page 109.

Discussion activity

With a partner, discuss what you think the phrase 'spiritual riches' means. Be prepared to share your ideas with others.

A A Buddhist monk

Christianity

The Bible teaches that all created things belong to God. People are given talents that should not be squandered. So it follows that talents can be used to earn money. But money, and in particular striving to acquire more than is needed, can take people's attention away from God and this is to be avoided.

Beliefs and teachings

No-one can serve two masters … You cannot serve both God and Money.

Matthew 6:24

Hinduism

Wealth may be a result of good karma in a previous life. If so, it is not a bad thing. Some would argue that the poor may have been wicked in a previous life and so are being punished in this one.

Islam

Wealth is a blessing from Allah and should be used to help others. The value of money is in what it can do, rather than what it is.

Beliefs and teachings

Richness does not lie in abundance of worldly goods, but true richness is the richness of the soul.

Hadith

Judaism

Wealth is permitted in Judaism, but must never take the place of God. Acquiring wealth may lead to sin, such as greed, selfishness and exploiting others, which must be guarded against.

Sikhism

Wealth may be a result of a previous life. Therefore it is not wrong in itself, but spiritual goals in life are much more important than wealth.

Beliefs and teachings

Blessed is the godly person and the riches they possess because they can be used for charitable purposes and to give happiness.

Guru Amar Das

Activities

1 Explain why equality in respect of money and possessions is impossible to achieve. Does this mean we should not try to achieve it? Why?

2 Do you think it is best for a religious person to be poor or rich? Explain your reasons.

3 Note down the attitudes to rich and poor, wealth and poverty of the religion(s) you are studying.

links

To find out more about religious attitudes to the responsible use of money, see pages 110–111.

Extension activity

'Responsible use of wealth is another way in which people can reach their spiritual goals.' Explain what you think this means.

Study tip

If referring to Christian attitudes, it may be helpful to use 1 Timothy 6:10, which says 'For the love of money is a root of all kinds of evil'. However, don't start the quotation with the word 'money' because this gives it a different meaning, which was not intended.

Summary

You should now be able to discuss religious attitudes towards the rich and the poor in society, and whether equality is achievable or desirable.

Why are some people rich?

Is being rich what you think it is?

Some people are so rich that they can live a life of luxury purely off the interest paid on their investments. They make money faster than they can spend it. However, most people have little opportunity of becoming extremely rich. Get-rich-quick schemes and long-lost relatives giving millions away are usually little more than fantasies.

Everyone probably knows of people who they think are a lot richer than they are. For example, the single mother living on benefits probably thinks that her landlord who rents out various properties, drives a smart car and holidays abroad is rich – certainly, he is in comparison to her, although even he may be struggling to meet all his financial commitments. So does everyone have the same idea of what it is to be rich?

Activities

1 How would you feel if you could make money faster than you can spend it?

2 If you could, would you be a better person than you are now? Explain the reasons for your answer.

3 How much money do you think you need to be called rich? Compare your idea with other people's.

Objectives

Understand that being rich is relative.

Identify and evaluate the ways people become rich.

Consider whether financial wealth contributes to the true worth of a person.

∞links

Look back at pages 100–101 to remind yourself about religious attitudes to the rich.

Key terms

Inheritance: when a friend or family member leaves you money or property in their will when they die.

Excessive salaries: also known as 'fat cat' salaries, large amounts of money earned, plus possibly bonuses and share options.

A Bill Gates – one of the world's wealthiest men

So how do people become rich?

There are many different ways in which someone could become rich. Some of them take a huge amount of effort and some none whatsoever.

- A relatively small minority of people are born into wealthy families and **inherit** a lot of money and/or wealth in possessions. However, no one can choose the family they are born into.

- Some people marry a rich spouse and share their wealth. If the spouse dies, the survivor may inherit all their money and possessions.

- Some people receive relative wealth through gifts, for example from older members of their family.

- A very few people win the lottery. The National Lottery has made over a thousand millionaires in Britain but, for every weekly winner, there are millions of people whose 'investment' of at least £1 might just as well have been thrown into the bin.

- Many people speculate on the financial markets. If the companies and products they invest in do well, investors can earn substantial returns of money. These people do not necessarily do anything to influence the company or product's success other than take the risk of investing their own money in it.

- A few inspired people make a lot of money by inventing a new product, marketing a new concept or creating something such as a popular song or a work of art. Songwriters receive a royalty payment every time their song is played commercially and inventors such as James Dyson earn more money every time their product is sold.

- Others have a talent for something that pays a good salary. If they are so talented or lucky that they receive national or international recognition, such as a film or football star, they may acquire vast amounts of money and possessions.

- Many people work extremely hard, probably for long hours, to earn enough to make them comfortably well off or wealthy. They may have studied hard over many years to get the type of job, for example as a lawyer or a doctor, that earns a high salary, or been very enterprising in growing a healthy business, such as a string of small shops.

- Saving and investing wisely also helps people to accumulate wealth. They might not become very rich, but certainly richer than they were.

∞ links

To read more about religious attitudes to Lotto winnings, see page 115.

B   *James Dyson, the multi-millionaire inventor of a bagless vacuum cleaner*

Study tip

You are expected to know of the causes and sources of wealth. If asked to explain these, you may find it useful to have thought about some examples.

Discussion activities

1. Who is more important – a top footballer, your teacher, the prime minister or a nurse? Choose one and, even though you may disagree, prepare an argument for that person being the most important. How does the amount of money they earn or the wealth they have relate to their importance? Be prepared to present your argument and answer questions.

2. Do you think it is morally right for some people in Britain to earn **excessive salaries** whilst others live in poverty?

3. For some people being rich is a dream; for others it is a nightmare. Some put it down to luck, some to talent and/or hard work. What do you think? Discuss it as a class.

Summary

You should now be able to discuss the ways in which people become rich and whether financial wealth is important in assessing the true worth of a person.

Poverty in Britain has many causes

There are many reasons why some people in Britain are poor. Often, poverty is a result of circumstances beyond the control of the people affected; occasionally, people make decisions that lead to their own poverty. Regardless of the cause, it is a commonly held belief that the poor need help to overcome their difficulties, which is often not easy to obtain. Below are four common reasons for poverty, although there are others.

Unemployment

Typically, there are between 1.5 million and 2 million people registered as unemployed in Britain, around 5–6% of the working population. In 2008, around 3 million families had no one in work and one in seven children lived in a household with no one in work. A significant number of people have illnesses or conditions that prevent them from working.

The unemployed claim benefits from the state, which provide enough to live on but not enough to give them a comfortable standard of living. In order to claim these benefits, they have to be actively seeking work. However, many lack the opportunities, education or skills to get the job they want or need. It is especially difficult for the homeless to get a job, as many employers are reluctant to take on someone without a home address or to trust a homeless person to be reliable. Homelessness can also prevent people from receiving state benefits.

There is also a minority of people who are too lazy or apathetic to work. If they are found out, the benefits they receive are likely to be reduced or even withdrawn.

Low wages

Despite the increased opportunities that education offers, there are millions of workers earning low wages. This is partly because many jobs do not require specialised skills and so they can be done by people with little or no training or ability. These jobs probably offer rates of pay at, or a little above, the national minimum wage, but this will provide barely sufficient to live and no luxuries. If the cost of food or basic necessities such as electricity rises faster than wages, these people will become poor.

> **Activity**
>
> Imagine you are the only wage earner and have a partner and small child. You need to provide a home, food and water, heating and lighting and items for your child. Your take-home pay (after income tax and National Insurance payments are deducted) is £1,000 a month. Write down how much you think you would need to spend every month on the items you need or want to ensure that you and your family can live.

> **Objectives**
>
> Know and understand various causes of poverty in Britain.

∞ links

Look back at pages 100–101 to remind yourself about religious attitudes to the poor.

∞ links

Read page 109 for more about the minimum wage.

A *Road sweepers earn very low wages*

■ Wasteful spending patterns

Some individuals earn what for many people would be a comfortable wage, but they spend a significant proportion of their money on tobacco, alcohol, gambling and/or other luxuries, leaving little or nothing for the basic necessities of life. This is especially hard on any children in the family, who are dependent on their parents fulfilling their responsibility to earn enough for their needs. They have no choice but to live in this way.

Chancellor's Budget increases: cigarettes up 15p per packet

Electricity to go up a further 10%

Shortage of wheat means bread will rise in price

■ Debt

Many people get themselves into serious debt through financial mismanagement. For example, they may be tempted to take out a credit card and use it to buy things they need or want, but are then not able to meet the monthly payments to reduce their debt. Others may be persuaded to borrow too much to buy a house only to struggle to meet the monthly mortgage payments. This could eventually lead to the bank or building society that loaned the money taking the house from them and leaving them homeless. The whole family may then be in poverty.

Some people do save and invest for their future, but occasionally investments go wrong and companies can fold, owing individuals or businesses thousands of pounds. Such a change in circumstances might reduce a person who had previously lived quite comfortably to being poor. In addition, they may have loans and credit agreements that they could previously pay off but now can no longer afford, leading them into worse debt.

Research activity 🔍

Look in a magazine or on the Internet for advertisements for credit cards or personal loans. Note down the rate of interest (APR rate) they charge. How might these rates contribute to a person being poor?

Discussion activity 👥

Discuss with a partner which of the four causes above is the most common cause of poverty in Britain. When you have decided, think about what could be done to help people affected by it. Write your answer down and be prepared to argue your case with others.

Study tip

If asked to give reasons why some people are poor, any of the reasons shown here will earn you marks.

Summary

You should now be able to discuss various causes of poverty.

Is this what poverty is all about?

A No home, no food – no hope?

No one to love, no one to care,
Nowhere to go, nowhere to stay,
The young man walks the streets,
Today as yesterday.
Passing time, relieving pain,
Nothing to lose, nothing to gain.

Activity

1 The above verse is about poverty and homelessness. Write your own verse of at least four lines which tells of your ideas about poverty in Britain.

Research activity

Find the song 'Streets of London' by Ralph McTell and either listen to it or read the lyrics.

The answer to the question in the sub heading above is 'maybe'. For some, the way of life portrayed in the verse is accurate. There are many homeless people begging on the streets, some in greater need than others. Those who do not find a place to sleep in a hostel have to sleep in the doorways of shops or in parks before they get moved on in the morning. Their few possessions travel the streets with them.

However, for many poor people, life is not quite so extreme. They may have a home – possibly small, run-down and in an area of town where they would prefer not to live – but at least it is somewhere they can call home. It may be cold in winter and food may not appear as regularly on the table as they would wish, but they may well have pride in it and do whatever they can to ensure they and their family do not go without too much. Although life is hard, many such families love and care for each other in a way that helps to make the physical hardships seem less significant.

Activities

2 In your opinion, do you think the two paragraphs above give a true picture of poverty in Britain? Explain why you think so. How would you give a more accurate picture?

3 Is pride and love more important than money? Give reasons for your opinion.

■ So who suffers most?

Children and young people are often the most badly affected by poverty because they are dependent on adults and can do nothing to raise their own standard of living. Teenagers could do a part-time job such as a paper round but, although this may give them pocket money and a degree of financial independence, it is unlikely to help the family's financial situation. They may suffer because their clothes are different, feel left out when their friends are discussing the latest 'must-have' mobile phone, games console, designer gear or music player and/or may be reluctant to invite friends round to their home.

However, the guilt and helplessness adults in the family may feel, especially if they are not to blame for the financial situation they and their family have to cope with, must not be underestimated. It is likely that they are aware that they may, through no fault of their own, be providing their children with a difficult start in life that they may struggle to overcome.

Young people who leave home in search of a better life often swap a poor but loving family for much worse. If they cannot get a job and escape poverty, such a move might result in a life of hardship on the streets, possibly leading to drug abuse or to prostitution as the only way of earning some money. In contrast, if they stay with or near their family and their desire to improve their life is planned and supported by the family, especially if that includes further education and/or training, there is a much better chance of success.

The elderly may also suffer particularly badly from poverty through not being able to work and provide money to make their state pensions go further. Coupled with frailty and possible ill health, their quality of life may be quite low.

Beliefs and teachings

Whoever in your kingdom is poor, to him let some help be given.

Cakkavatti Sihanada Sutta

Beliefs and teachings

God's bounty belongs to all, but in this world it is not shared justly.

Adi Granth 1171

Activity

4　Which of these groups suffers most, and least, from poverty in Britain? Put them in order and explain your reasons:

a　children

b　adults

c　young people

d　elderly people.

Extension activity

In your opinion, what can be done to reduce poverty in Britain? Would this be fair, and, if so, to whom?

Study tip

If you give an opinion in an examination answer, make sure you support it with reasons you can fully explain.

Summary

You should now be able to discuss the effects of poverty, especially in relation to particular groups in British society.

■ The chances of escaping the poverty trap

Many extremely poor people in Britain cannot escape the **poverty trap**. They may live in socially deprived areas or on the streets. Without resources or confidence, they find that getting an education, qualifications, skills and a good job is just too difficult. However, some do succeed in lifting themselves out of that situation. Although they may not become very rich, they may be able to provide a comfortable standard of living for themselves and their family.

A few overcome poverty to become extremely rich. For example, some wealthy businesspeople and successful sports and entertainment stars started their careers with very little, but through talent, hard work, initiative and/or luck have amassed great fortunes.

Objectives

Understand ways in which poverty may be overcome.

Evaluate the effectiveness of these ways.

Beliefs and teachings

How long will you lie there, you sluggard? When will you get up from your sleep? … poverty will come on you like a bandit and scarcity like an armed man.

Proverbs 6:9 and 11

Activity

1
  a Do you think the above description of life for a young person in a socially deprived area is an accurate one? Give your reasons.

  b What other factors would you add to the description?

  c What skills and resources do you think are needed to break out of the poverty trap?

A   *Sir Alan Sugar, a very wealthy businessman*

■ Education and training

Many young people benefit from the education offered in schools, with support and encouragement from their families and teachers. They gain qualifications that lead to further education, good careers and a comfortable way of life.

Others find it difficult to benefit from school. Some have too many problems and less support at home; others do not understand the difference education could make to their lives. They leave without gaining many or any qualifications. Unskilled, low-paid work may be the best they can hope for.

Education does not need to stop after school. There are courses in literacy and numeracy, as well as vocational skills such as bricklaying, on a full- or a part-time basis. Vocational courses include work in local businesses. Alternatively, many companies pay for young workers to

Key terms

Poverty trap: not being able to break out of poverty.

Minimum wage: the legal minimum amount which must be paid to a worker in the UK.

attend college part-time to improve their skills. For those who need to earn money while studying, this route to education and training may be a good option. Students attending college between the ages of 16 and 19 receive a maintenance allowance (depending on their parents' salaries).

Counselling

Many young people need extra help to make career choices or decisions that may affect their standard of living. Schools and colleges have specialist careers advisers and the local-authority-based Connexions service gives advice on such areas as careers, learning, health, housing, money and rights.

Adults can also obtain advice that may help to lift them out of poverty. The Citizens Advice service is a national charity with 3,200 offices, providing free advice on social, legal, financial and other issues.

Government help

Many people look to the government for help. As a society, we expect government to pass laws to protect the poor and provide benefits to help them survive. We can vote for the political party that we think will help most and we pay our taxes to provide the necessary resources.

In 1999, the British government introduced a **minimum wage** to prevent workers being exploited by being paid too little. From 1 October 2008, a full-time worker over the age of 22 had to be paid at least £5.73 per hour (rates for younger workers were less). For a 40-hour working week this amounted to (after deduction of income tax and National Insurance payments) pay of nearly £200 per week. This applied to around 2,500,000 people, mostly in unskilled or semi-skilled jobs.

The government also provides benefits to help individuals and families, including:

- unemployment benefit, to help the family of someone seeking a job
- invalidity benefit, to help the family of someone who cannot work due to a specified illness
- an allowance for every family to contribute towards the extra costs of raising children
- financial assistance with accommodation and council tax
- tax credits, which reduce the amount of income tax low earners pay
- old age pension for all those over retirement age who have made sufficient National Insurance contributions.

Activity

2 'The minimum wage should be much higher.' What do you think? Give your reasons.

∞ links

To find out about the work of charities and religious organisations in helping the poor, see pages 110–113.

B *Many individuals and families claim benefits from the government*

Study tip

If referring to a state benefit in an answer, it is good to give an example.

Summary

You should now be able to discuss and evaluate the ways in which poverty might be overcome. You should also understand why some people can and others cannot break out of the poverty trap.

Activity

3 **a** List different ways in which the poor can be helped. Compare your list with someone else's and add to it if necessary.

   b Spend five minutes thinking about it and then explain what you think can be done to improve our present system of supporting the poor.

General principles

All religions teach that people should use their wealth responsibly. Theistic religions teach that wealth is a gift and God expects people to use it to help others, as well as themselves. That does not mean that only rich people should help the poor, but that everyone has a duty not to be greedy and selfish but to help others less fortunate than themselves. In the first instance, people might help other members of their own family. They might also help their local community, giving their time and money to support specific projects. Many people also give money to support the work of charities helping individuals, families and communities in Britain and abroad.

Religions teach that responsible use of money helps a person's spiritual growth. Along with performing religious observances (e.g. prayer), it will help them to earn good karma or to be seen as worthy of entering heaven. Many believers, and also non-believers, teach their children from a young age that it is a good thing to raise or save money to donate to **charity** and help the less fortunate.

Activity

1 Invent a case study for a person who was born into a wealthy British family, but who was poor by the time they were 30. Write at least 25 lines, explaining how they lost their wealth and the effects of the change on their life.

What each religion teaches

Buddhism

Buddhists believe that excess wealth should be given to the poor so the giver can earn good karma. The Eightfold Path advises that extremes of poverty and wealth ought to be avoided, so excess wealth should be used to help eliminate poverty. The first of the six perfections requires generosity in giving.

Christianity

Christianity teaches that excess wealth should be shared with the poor. Most church communities, including youth organisations, get involved in raising money to support charity work. Christians remember Jesus teaching his followers that the poor would always be with them and that people should do what they can to help them. He told several rich people, either directly or in parables, to give their riches to the poor. He also praised a poor widow for giving a tiny amount (which she probably could not afford) to the poor, saying she had in fact given more than the rich who had given larger amounts. He said this is the way to build 'riches in heaven'.

Objectives

Investigate religious attitudes toward the responsible use of money.

Consider how much wealth rich people should give away.

Key terms

Charity: giving to the needy.

⊂⊃ links

To find out more about the work religious charities do to help the poor, see pages 112–113.

A *Hereford Cathedral needs to spend a lot of money on restoration of the building*

Discussion activity

In pairs, discuss why Jesus praised the poor widow for giving a small amount. Look at Luke 21:1–4 to help you.

Hinduism

Wealth should be shared and not hoarded. It is a daily duty to show hospitality to the poor by helping them. Some Hindus give food to at least one poor person before they eat their own midday meal, or give money to beggars.

Islam

Islam teaches that the value of money is in what it can do, rather than in what it is. Muslims believe that because wealth is a blessing from Allah, it should be used wisely for the benefit of the poor, as well as for oneself. Often families will help each other to provide assistance with business opportunities and interest-free loans. Zakah, the third pillar, ensures that all Muslims give 2.5% of their wealth to the poor every year. Voluntary Sadaqah encourages giving extra.

Judaism

The Torah contains many laws to protect the poor and vulnerable, and Judaism teaches that some of a person's wealth must be given to help the community. Jews give to charity through tzedakah out of a sense of justice and righteousness. This is supposed to be 10% of their income per year, although interpretations of this figure vary. Jewish children are encouraged to collect coins in a box called a pushke and then give them to the poor.

B   *Jewish children save money in a pushke to give to charity*

Sikhism

Sikhs believe that everyone should have access to the necessities of life and that the wealthy have a responsibility to try to make sure this happens. Providing assistance for family members is important. They give vand chhakna out of a sense of collective responsibility for each other. This is related to the idea of sewa – service to others.

Study tip

If you are writing about two religions, make sure that you make it clear that you know that their beliefs on this topic are similar, whilst taking care to point out any differences that do exist.

Activity

2   What are the advantages and disadvantages of insisting that people give a minimum amount to charity rather than allowing them to choose whether and how much to give? Is setting a percentage amount the best way? Give your reasons.

Extension activity

'Christians should insist that the Church gives all its wealth to the poor.' What do you think? Why?

Research activity

Look up the following Bible references for Jesus's teaching: Luke 18:18–25; Luke 19:1–10; Luke 21:1–4.

Summary

You should now be able to discuss religious attitudes to the responsible use of money, and some specific ways in which believers should try to help the less fortunate.

What are the options?

Most people, whether religious or not, agree that we should look after the poor in our society. Taxpayers pay their taxes so that local government can provide some types of care on behalf of us all. Families may be in a position to help poorer family members. Other people raise or donate money to charities and religious organisations to support the work they do with the poor in our communities.

Beliefs and teachings

Love your neighbour as yourself.
Luke 10:27

Do not do to another what you do not like to be done to yourself.
Mahabharata

Local authorities

Local authorities have a responsibility to care for the poor and vulnerable in our communities. The services they provide include:

- social workers to assist individuals and families in need or at risk
- people to advise the poor on how best to provide for themselves and their families
- support workers to give practical help to the elderly and others who find it difficult to cope on their own.

Local authorities also provide houses or flats for rent, which is subsidised through housing benefit if a person cannot afford it. However, there is only a limited supply of accommodation and long waiting lists, with the people and especially families judged to be the most in need nearest the top. Factors for prioritising include whether the family has young children or the applicant has become homeless to escape domestic violence. The ability to pay is not considered.

Discussion activity

With a partner, discuss whether a lone parent who has three children and cannot find a job should be given council accommodation more quickly than someone without children, who is working full-time. Try to look at more than one side of the issue and be prepared to share your ideas.

Charities and religious organisations

Charities also offer practical support to the poor. This includes collecting and redistributing second-hand clothes and household goods to families in need, supporting children (e.g. the National Society for the Prevention of Cruelty to Children (NSPCC) and the Children's Society) and supporting the elderly (Help the Aged). Some charities, such as the Salvation Army, are run by religious organisations.

Charities are very much dependent on the generosity of ordinary people, many of whom raise funds and donate money to keep the

Objectives

Know and understand the roles of different individuals and organisations in caring for the poor.

Understand religious beliefs about the responsibility for the care of the poor.

⬭ links

'Housing benefit' is defined in the Glossary at the back of this book.

Key terms

Charity: an organisation that does not work for profit and which usually works to help others.

Research activity

Find out more about the work of the Salvation Army. Start with www.salvationarmy.org.uk.

charity work going and/or devote their own time to work voluntarily. Religious people might see their involvement as a vocation or a calling from God. Some charities also receive money from the National Lottery. However, charities can provide help only for as long as the money comes in. If the money runs out, the work stops.

links

See pages 114–115 for more on Lottery funding for charity.

Case study

Telford in Shropshire, like every other town in the country, has a problem with homelessness. Telford Christian Council, a charity that works in partnership with the local council, runs a hostel called Wesley House. The hostel is in an old Methodist chapel and provides short-term accommodation for up to eight young homeless people. The charity also manages a further 89 units of short-term supported accommodation across Telford. The small team of staff are able to assess homeless people's needs and outline the options available to them. In a typical month, they will deal with around 50 referrals, all homeless people between the ages of 16 and 25, who urgently need somewhere to live.

B *Wesley House, Telford – a hostel for the homeless*

■ Families

Many people say that relatives should help family members who fall on hard times. Whilst in many cases this actually happens, in others it is not possible. Some people are in need because of a breakdown in the family itself. There can be many reasons for this type of breakdown, which can happen in poor and wealthy families, and these include abuse, arguments with partners and addiction. However, most families who are considered to be financially poor manage to provide enough to ensure that the family home is stable and offers support when needed. A family unit can be successful even if it has only just enough money for necessities such as food, clothes and shelter.

links

Look back at pages 110–111 to remind yourself about religious attitudes to the responsible use of money.

Activity

1 a Note down and explain the alternative sources of support for the poor.

b Give your thoughts on each of these sources. Which do you think is best and worst? Are there other ways of getting help? Is enough support available? Should more or less be provided? Explain your reasons.

c What advice would you give to a friend who tells you that they regularly feel hungry because there is too little food at home?

Summary

You should now be able to discuss various ways in which the poor can be helped.

The Lottery is born

On 19 November 1994, after much advance publicity and months of preparation, the **National Lottery** was drawn live on national television for the first time. The first draw had seven jackpot winners, winning around £840,000 each. The first 'lottery millionaires' were created in the second draw, with four people winning around £1.76 million each. They had correctly selected the six winning numbers and paid £1 for those numbers to be registered on their ticket. Since that day, the National Lottery has grown dramatically, first with a second weekly draw on Wednesdays, then with a special 'Thunderball' draw and even special draws in support of the London 2012 Olympics. A European lottery draw (Euromillions) was started and, because it is more difficult to win than the ordinary draw, the jackpot regularly 'rolls over'. A first prize approaching £100 million has been won on several occasions for a stake of £1.50 (2 euros). In addition, people also face the temptation of buying instant 'scratch-card' tickets where the majority of the prizes are very small and are paid out straightaway by the retailer.

Many critics have argued that the National Lottery is nothing more than an extra voluntary tax paid by the poor in the vain hope of winning enough to take them out of the poverty trap. After all, the rich have no need to buy a ticket because, although winning would be nice, it would not have such a dramatic effect on their lives. In addition, there is debate about the risk of an 'unsuitable' person winning. There have been instances in which convicted criminals or people whose behaviour is antisocial end up with many millions of pounds which many people feel they don't deserve and/or can't cope with.

A *Is the Lotto a good thing?*

Objectives

Understand different attitudes to the Lottery.

Reflect on the benefits of Lotto money supporting good causes.

Key terms

National Lottery (Lotto): regular gambling competition, available to all over-16s and which offers large prizes, but also gives money to charity. 'Lotto' is now its official name.

Discussion activity

Discuss with a partner what you would do if, at the age of 16, you won £5 million on the Lottery. How would you spend the money?

Activities

1 Explain why some people are in favour of playing the National Lottery and some are against it.

2 Who, if anyone, would be an 'unsuitable' winner? Give your reasons.

■ Money to good causes

One of the big 'selling points' is that, for every £1 staked on the National Lottery, 28 pence is given to 'good causes'. Currently, over £21 billion have been distributed to these good causes. This has to be bid for and there are strict rules about who or what can benefit. There are four categories of good cause:

- arts (16.67%)
- heritage (16.67%)
- sport (16.67%)
- health, education, the environment and charitable expenditure (50%).

Whilst most people approve of at least some of these categories, some grants have attracted criticism. For example, large grants have been made to the Royal Opera House and the British Museum, which some people do not think are worthy causes because they do not benefit the poor. On the other hand, lots of smaller grants have been given to help local community and charity projects to help the poor.

■ Religious attitudes to the National Lottery

Buddhist, Hindu, Jewish, Islamic and Sikh teachings forbid any form of gambling, including the National Lottery, as it is seen as a way of earning money that does not involve doing honest work, and can promote greed and encourage laziness. Money should be used for the necessities of life and not for speculating to win more. For every person who becomes richer as a result of gambling, many others become poorer. These five religions will not bid for lottery funding for projects supported by their faith, whether it is for the upkeep of places of worship or to support charity organisations they run.

Some Christian denominations (e.g. Methodists) share these views on gambling, but other denominations (Church of England, Roman Catholics), whilst not actively encouraging gambling, will allow believers to gamble in moderation. 'Good causes' funds have been used by some Christian charities and the Heritage Fund has provided finance for the upkeep of churches and cathedrals.

Beliefs and teachings

Do not wear yourself out to get rich; have the wisdom to show restraint.

Proverbs 23:4

Beliefs and teachings

Wine and games of chance are abominations devised by Satan. Avoid them, so that you may prosper.

Qur'an 5:90

Beliefs and teachings

He alone has found the right way who eats what he earns through toil and shares his earnings with the needy.

Guru Granth Sahib 1245

Activity

3   Rank the 4 categories of good causes, with the one you think is most worthy at the top and the least worthy at the bottom. Explain your choice of the most and least worthy. You could discuss this with a partner first.

Extension activity

Research the work of a voluntary organisation which has benefited from Lottery funding.

Activities

4   Note down the attitude to the National Lottery of the religion you are studying.

5   What do you think about the National Lottery, both as a form of gambling and as a way of providing funds for worthy causes? Give your reasons.

Summary

You should now be able to discuss different attitudes towards the National Lottery, the funding it gives and the morality of this type of gambling.

Case study

£10 million winner

In January 1997, John McGuinness, a hospital porter earning around £150 per week, won just over £10 million on the National Lottery. Eleven years later, his personal wealth had gone and he was deep in debt and looking for work. His house had been repossessed and luxury items such as cars, jewellery and a holiday villa were sold in order to meet some of his debts.

The main cause of his downfall was his investment in his favourite football team – Livingston FC. He used his fortune to guarantee loans made to the club and, when the club went bankrupt, he found himself owing millions of pounds to creditors – money he no longer had.

What John McGuinness spent	
£4 million	Livingston Football Club
£2.5 million	Gifts to family members
£750,000	Gift to ex-wife
£500,000	New home
£500,000	Spanish apartment
£500,000	Cars
£500,000	Charities
£200,000	Wedding
£250,000	Holidays
£150,000	Jewellery for his wife

Commenting on his downfall, John McGuinness said:

'I probably was a bit naive and perhaps made a mistake ... I just want my life to get back to the way it was before – but minus the football ... I have learned a great deal from the experience, which I suppose is a positive thing to take out of it.'

A Lottery winner John McGuinness

Case study

Muslim winner

In December 1994, Mukhtar Mohidin, a Muslim from Blackburn, won £17.9 million on the National Lottery. Despite trying to keep his win secret, news about it leaked out. The problem was that, according to Muslim beliefs about gambling, Mukhtar should not have bought a lottery ticket in the first place.

Mukhtar decided to provide £300,000 for a community centre to be built alongside the Masjid Al Momineen Mosque. However, in 1998, after the foundations and steelwork had been completed, the project ground to a halt when it was discovered that most of the funding had come from Mukhtar's lottery winnings. No other Muslim source of funding will pay for it to be completed because of this.

Salim Mulla, the secretary of the Lancashire Council of Mosques, was quoted as saying: 'As Muslims, we are not allowed to accept money from gambling. Clean money is what people have worked for, not got from gambling, betting or the Lottery'.

Whilst Mukhtar is still able to enjoy his winnings, he has changed his name and moved away from his friends and family. In 1998, after court battles caused by some family members trying to claim some of his fortune, his wife Sayeeda divorced him after 17 years of marriage.

B　*The part-built community centre*

Beliefs and teachings

No one eats better food than that which they have earned with their own labours.

Hadith

∞ links

Look back at 110–111 to remind yourself of religious attitudes to the responsible use of money.

Study tip

You can use either of these case studies, or any others you know of, as examples to support the points you make.

Summary

You should now know about the experiences of two lottery winners and explored the consequences of how they spent their winnings.

Activities

3 a　Do you think the Muslim community was right to refuse to accept money from Mukhtar's winnings? Give reasons for your opinion.

　　b　Do you think that Mukhtar regrets winning the Lottery? Give reasons for your opinion.

4　'The National Lottery is not really gambling – it's just a bit of fun.' What do you think? Explain your opinion.

5

Religious attitudes to the rich and the poor in British society – summary

For the examination you should now be able to:

✔ know and understand religious beliefs and teachings concerning individual wealth and poverty

✔ know and understand explanations for the existence of both rich and poor in society

✔ understand and discuss religious attitudes to rich and poor and to the responsible use of money

✔ understand the causes and sources of wealth

✔ understand the possible causes of poverty and ways of overcoming poverty

✔ understand and evaluate the effects of the minimum wage and excessive salaries

✔ understand who is responsible for the poor, including the roles of the state, the community and the family, and what they should do to care for the poor

✔ understand and evaluate the role of lotteries as a source of charity funding and personal wealth.

Sample answer

1 Write an answer to the following exam question:
Explain how the National Lottery can help the poor.

(4 marks)

2 Read the following sample answer:

> The National Lottery can help the poor by letting people win millions. It only costs £1 for a ticket and you could win £5 million or more. This will stop that person and their family being poor. If you win, you could even give a bit of it to charity.

3 With a partner, discuss the sample answer. Do you think that there are other things the student could have included in the answer?

4 What mark would you give this answer out of 4? Look at the mark scheme in the Introduction on page 7 (AO1). What are the reasons for the mark you have given?

Practice questions

1   Look at the photograph below and answer the following questions.

(a) Give two reasons why a person might be poor.   *(4 marks)*

Study tip As you are being asked to give two reasons, make sure you include some detail for each one.

(b) Explain why some religious people feel they should help the poor.   *(3 marks)*

Study tip Make sure you include some religious teaching and perhaps a quotation in your answer.

(c) 'No religious person should be rich.' What do you think? Explain your opinion.   *(3 marks)*

Study tip Your opinion is worth credit only if you support it with reasons.

(d) Explain briefly the meaning of 'the poverty trap'.   *(2 marks)*

Study tip To answer a question like this, say what 'poverty trap' means and give some detail to support your definition.

(e) 'The minimum wage should be much higher.' Do you agree? Give reasons and explain your answer, showing you have thought about more than one point of view. Refer to religious arguments in your answer.   *(6 marks)*

Study tip Even though the quotation in this final question does not include any religious reference, you need to include arguments from a religious perspective to gain more than three marks.

6.1 The scale of world poverty

Activity

1   Imagine that your nearest source of drinking water is a dirty stream two miles from where you live. The water carries disease but there is nothing else to drink. What do you do? Explain why.

Objectives

Appreciate the effect poverty has on the world.

Understand that there are inequalities in the world which lead to extreme poverty in some countries.

As you sit in your classroom, possibly with a bottle of drinking water on your table or in your bag, there are millions of people in some parts of the world whose daily routine will be to go to their nearest stream and bring back enough water for their family to use. They may even have a wash in the stream before they collect the water from it. After all, other people and animals do exactly that. For them, a bottle of clean, pure chilled water seems an impossible dream.

This, of course, makes them susceptible to diseases such as cholera and dysentery that are carried in dirty water, but, as there is no alternative, it is a risk worth taking. But why should millions of people have to take this risk?

Discussion activity

With a partner, think about why billions of people in the world have to risk drinking dirty water.

In addition, people in these parts of the world are likely to struggle to grow sufficient food to provide for themselves and their families. Consequently their life expectancy is much lower than ours is in Britain.

Beliefs and teachings

Be grateful to God whose bounties you enjoy. Be compassionate to the needy and the people you employ.

Guru Nanak

A *Everyone needs fresh water to survive*

As the map shows, there are large areas of the world, mainly between the tropics of Cancer and Capricorn, in which states are described as **less economically developed countries** (LEDCs). The fact that they are less economically developed means they are considered to be poor. Richer countries are referred to as **economically developed countries** (EDCs) and tend to be north or south of the tropics.

Beliefs and teachings

Thus, from the not giving of property to the needy, poverty became widespread.

Digha-Nikaya III, 65

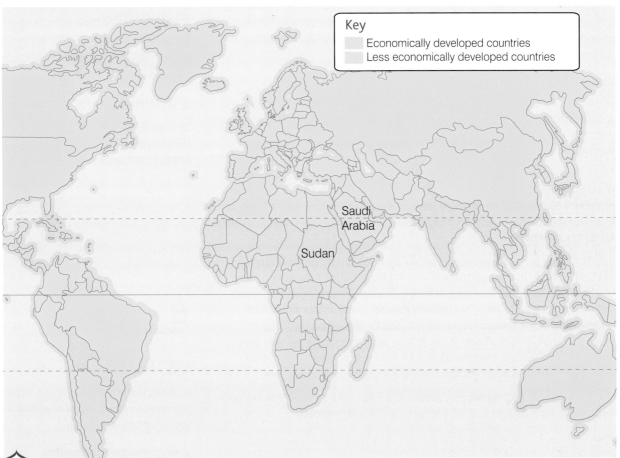

Key
- Economically developed countries
- Less economically developed countries

Saudi Arabia

Sudan

B *The economically developed and less economically developed countries around the world*

Activity

2 Why do you think LEDCs tend to be between the tropics on either side of the equator, whilst EDCs are either north or south of the tropics? Explain your answer.

Research activity

Find out the names of six less economically developed countries and six economically developed countries, and locate them on a map. Apart from poverty, are there other things that the LEDCs have in common?

Key terms

Less economically developed country (LEDC): a poor country, where people live in poverty.

Economically developed country (EDC): a rich country where people enjoy a comfortable standard of living.

Summary

You should now understand that billions of people, chiefly in less economically developed countries (LEDCs), live in poverty without clean drinking water or sufficient food.

Study tip

Remember, Africa is a continent, not a country.

Introduction

There are several reasons why some countries in the world are affected by poverty. Some reasons are linked to natural causes, whilst others are influenced by people, often in richer and more economically developed countries. We are going to look at how some of these factors affect two different countries – Saudi Arabia and Sudan.

Location

A country's geographical location can affect its wealth. This may be partially due to its climate but also to whether it has natural resources such as oil and gold, which richer countries want to buy.

Countries in the Middle East, such as Saudi Arabia, have a climate that is very hot and dry – the sort of climate that would normally lead to poverty. However, because they have large reserves of oil within their boundaries, they are very wealthy. Saudi Arabia has 25% of the world's oil so far discovered.

Saudi Arabia is separated from Sudan by a relatively narrow stretch of the Red Sea, but, as pictures B and C show, Saudi Arabia is a rich country due to its oil reserves, whereas Sudan is very poor. Although the two countries have very similar climates, Sudan has much less oil and few other natural resources. In 2006, the gross national income (GNI), which shows how rich or poor a country is, was $640 per person in Sudan, compared to $11,770 per person in its richer neighbour Saudi Arabia (in the United Kingdom it was $37,600).

The average life expectancy in Sudan is 57 for men and 60 for women, whilst in Saudi Arabia it is 71 for men and 75 for women.

B *A refugee camp in Sudan*

Objectives

Investigate some causes of world poverty.

Compare the neighbouring countries of Saudi Arabia and Sudan.

∞links

To read about how climate can contribute to the problem of poverty, see page 124.

A *Neighbouring countries Saudi Arabia and Sudan*

∞links

Look back at the map on page 121 if you need to check Saudi Arabia and Sudan's positions globally.

Study tip

The picture(s) on your examination paper should help you to focus on the topic.

Natural disasters

The geographical location of a country can also make it more or less prone to **natural disasters** such as earthquakes, volcano eruptions, severe drought or tidal flooding. Although these disasters hit both LEDCs and EDCs, developed countries have more money, resources and expertise to help them deal with the effects and recover more quickly. LEDCs do not have these advantages.

Politics and corruption

Saudi Arabia and Sudan are also different because of their political situations. Whilst Saudi Arabia has a relatively stable government, Sudan is not stable. There has been **civil war** in the Darfur region in western Sudan for around 25 years. This conflict has cost the lives of at least 200,000 people and caused around 2 million others to flee their homes. Despite the peace deal signed in 2005, there is evidence that pro-government militias have been carrying out ethnic cleansing, killing non-Arab groups in Darfur.

Corruption is another factor that contributes to the problem of poverty. In unstable countries there are sometimes a few rich people in central or regional government who keep money for themselves rather than allowing it to benefit the poor.

C   *Riyadh in Saudi Arabia. Saudi Arabia has benefitted enormously from its oil reserves.*

Activity

Draw a chart like the one below. Add facts about the location, climate, resources, wealth, life expectancy and politics.

	Saudi Arabia	Sudan
Location		
Climate		
Resources		
Wealth		
Life expectancy		
Politics		

Key terms

Natural disaster: a disaster caused by nature, e.g. earthquakes, volcanoes.

Civil war: a war fought against a country's government by people living within that country.

Corruption: dishonesty that usually leads to the accumulation of wealth.

∞links

Turn to pages 134–135 to find about the cyclone disaster in Burma.

Summary

You should now be able to discuss some of the reasons that may cause a country to be rich or poor and understand that whilst some are natural, others are caused by people.

Climate

One of the biggest causes of poverty is **climate**. In order to grow crops to eat or to feed animals, a certain amount of rainfall is needed. However, 92% of the African continent, including countries such as Somalia and Chad, has insufficient rainfall when it is needed. Summers are very hot, baking the arid land and making it impossible to plant, water and grow crops. Such conditions mean there is also not enough water for people to drink. Because the countries are poor, they do not have the facilities to collect and keep the water that falls during the rainy season for when it is needed.

Scientists estimate that global warming is making matters worse. The dry regions are becoming drier and the wet regions wetter. This trend is likely to continue, resulting in millions of people facing the prospect of starvation unless rich countries provide them with food. In 2006, over 25 million people in African countries south of the Sahara faced a food crisis. That figure is rising year on year. It is ironic that the countries that are suffering most from climate change are contributing least to global warming.

Population growth

Another cause of poverty is population growth, especially in those countries that can least afford extra mouths to feed. Population growth tends to be greater in poor countries where there is a lack of contraception and where, because many babies die in infancy, people tend to have more children anyway to ensure they have someone to care for them in later life.

Objectives

Investigate some further causes of world poverty.

Understand and evaluate some of the problems caused by world poverty.

Key terms

Climate: the regular weather conditions of an area.

World trade: different countries buying and selling goods from/to each other.

Global interdependence: where different countries in the world are dependent upon each other for trade and survival.

Study tip

You will not be expected to quote figures, but it will help if you show that you know that there are big differences between countries.

Country	Number of live births per thousand that die by their 5th birthday
Mali	199.7
Somalia	192.8
Chad	189.0
The world	73.7
United Kingdom	6.0

B   Source: United Nations Population Division

A   Population growth can put a strain on essential resources, such as clean drinking water, especially in poorer countries

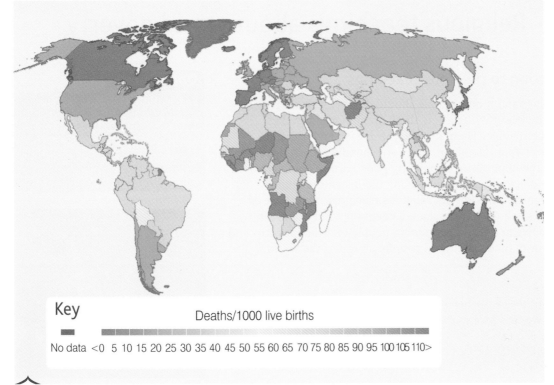

Key   Deaths/1000 live births

No data <0 5 10 15 20 25 30 35 40 45 50 55 60 65 70 75 80 85 90 95 100 105 110>

C   *Infant mortality rates around the world, 2007 (Source: CIA World Factbook 2007)*

Economic reasons – world trade

The **world trade** system, which governs what countries buy and sell to each other and the price they are able to charge, does nothing to help most inhabitants of poorer countries. Producers of crops such as wheat and rice sell their crops to the country that pays the most. Because poor countries cannot afford to pay these prices, they have to depend on what they can produce themselves. However, self-production in these countries is hindered by wealthy farmers using valuable agricultural land to grow cash crops such as fruit and vegetables that they can sell to rich countries. So the land is not being used to grow crops that would feed the poor, and the profit the landowner makes does not help the poor either.

But every country needs to trade with other countries for those items they cannot produce themselves. This is an aspect of **global interdependence**. Very often, LEDCs buy products they need but at market prices that they cannot really afford, which leads them into debt. These debts mount up massively and high interest rates only make the countries even poorer. Some people would argue that this system amounts to the exploitation of LEDCs.

Activities

1. In this and the previous unit, we have identified five reasons why countries are poor (location, politics, climate, population growth and economics). Put these reasons in order of importance. Explain your ranking of the most and the least important reasons.

2. Which of these five causes do you think is easiest to solve? Explain how you think it could be solved.

3. 'Rich countries should help poor countries.' What do you think? Explain your opinion.

Summary

You should now be able to discuss why climate, population growth and economics are all reasons why some countries are poor.

Introduction to religious teachings

Religious teachings about how people should deal with world poverty are based on principles that believers think are important in the treatment of other people. These include the Jewish and Christian imperative to 'love your neighbour' and corresponding teachings from other religions: the importance of building good karma, doing good things to earn a place in heaven and saving life instead of killing – not harming life (ahimsa). In addition, religious teachings, and those of secular humanists, tell us that we share a common bond of humanity, even though we live in a world containing people of different races and faiths. So it is our duty to care for all people, all round the world.

Specific religious teachings

Buddhism

Wealth has to be earned honestly (right livelihood) and this is an acceptable goal provided it does not cause others to suffer. Wealth should be used for others, however, and not hoarded. Generosity creates good karma. Craving wealth creates greed, which leads to suffering and too much attachment to the world. Giving money away prevents people from becoming attached to their wealth. Therefore, wealth should be used to allow others to have the necessities of life.

Christianity

The main teaching is to 'love your neighbour as yourself', which introduces the parable of the good Samaritan (Luke 10:25–37). The parable teaches Christians that people in need must be helped, even if they are from a different race or religion. Spending life obsessively gaining money prevents a Christian from getting close to God or showing their love for God. Instead, money should be used to help the poor and homeless. There are many Christian charities working throughout the world (e.g. Christian Aid, CAFOD, Tearfund, World Vision) to help the poor.

Hinduism

Hindus are encouraged to earn wealth honestly by lawful means. This enables them to share with the poor as a way of earning good karma. Hindus have to observe Dharma, which is righteous duty and includes

Objectives

Learn about religious teachings relating to world poverty.

Evaluate how well these teachings relate to world poverty.

A

Study tip

In your exam, try to include specific teachings from the religion(s) you have studied along with more general ones.

Beliefs and teachings

Look upon the world as a...mirage [an illusion]... for the wise there is no attachment at all.

Dhammapada 170–1

Beliefs and teachings

You cannot serve both God and Money.

Matthew 6:24

Beliefs and teachings

Be kind and charitable towards the deserving ones.

Shikshapatri

helping the poor. Many British Hindus support charitable projects, especially those working in India.

Islam

Wealth is given by Allah for the good of all humanity and therefore should be shared. Giving to charity is not voluntary. Zakah (2.5% of savings) has to be given every year and extra giving (sadaqah) is encouraged. Charging interest on loans (which could be seen as exploitation) is forbidden in Islam. This helps the poor by reducing repayments and preventing debt. If repayments cannot be made, the loan can become a gift. Logically, this may be extended to debts to Islamic governments accumulated by LEDCs. Islamic charities and relief organisations such as the Red Crescent and Islamic Relief provide worldwide help.

Beliefs and teachings

He who eats and drinks whilst his brother goes hungry is not one of us.

Hadith

Judaism

Jews believe that, as all wealth comes from God, it should be shared with those who do not have a fair share. Any Jew anywhere has the right to live in Israel, so many escape poverty in this way. The prophets who lived between the 7th and 4th centuries BCE (e.g. Amos) warned that those who built great wealth through exploiting the poor would be punished. The book of Deuteronomy instructs Jews to cancel debt every seven years. This requirement from God could be interpreted as an instruction for the debts LEDCs have accumulated to be cancelled by the rich countries who loaned the money.

Beliefs and teachings

You trample on the poor and force him to give you grain …
Seek good, not evil, that you may live.

Amos 5:11–14

Sikhism

One of the key ideas in Sikhism is service (sewa). This can be physical service (tan), mental service (man), such as studying how to help others, and material service (dhan), such as giving money to help others. Sewa is practised in the langar (kitchen) in every gurdwara, which provides a free meal for whomever wants it, whatever their religion or nationality.

Beliefs and teachings

A place in God's court can only be attained if we do service to others in this world.

Adi Granth 26

Activity

4   Note down the religious teachings about world poverty from the religion(s) you are studying.

Extension activity

1   Look at the book of Amos and consider the prophet's teaching on religion and wealth (e.g. Amos 2:6; 5:11–15, 21–24).

Research activity

Find out about the Jewish charity Tzedek on www.tzedek.org.uk.

Extension activity

2   Look at the beliefs and teachings for each religion. Explain what you think each quotation means, in the context of world poverty, to a believer in the religion(s) you are studying.

Summary

You should now be able to discuss how major religions teach their followers about the importance of helping the poor.

6.5   Justice, stewardship and compassion

The key to triumphing over evil

In the 18th century, British politician Edmund Burke made the following statement:

> 66 *All that is necessary for the triumph of evil is for good people to do nothing.* 99

Three important concepts – **justice**, **stewardship** and **compassion** – depend on people actually doing something in order to help the fight against poverty

Activity

1 Explain what you think Edmund Burke meant in his statement. Do you agree with it? Give reasons for your opinion.

Justice

Justice is often portrayed as a set of balanced scales. It is related to fairness. If something is just, it is considered to be fair to all parties. If it is unfair to one side or the other, it is called unjust. Whilst the term 'justice' is often used in relation to a criminal trial, it has a wider application. The fact that many people in LEDCs do not have access to clean water and some are dying of starvation is clearly unjust, because it is unfair.

In religious belief, theistic religions teach that God is completely just. In other words, God is seen as totally fair in all his dealings with his creation – all are valued equally. It can therefore be assumed that world poverty offends against God's sense of justice.

Stewardship

The word 'steward' is used in various contexts. A flight assistant is often called an air steward or stewardess and is in charge of people's comfort and safety. A 'steward' is someone in charge of something valuable for someone else and who is involved in caring responsibly. Traditionally, a steward in a household was the person in charge of the property and the finances. Often stewards worked for lords or landowners – they were expected to run things properly on the owner's behalf and make sure that everything was looked after well.

In a religious sense, the idea of stewardship is taken from the creation story. All theistic religions believe that the earth was created by God. As part of this, humans were created in order to look after the earth for God. This is a special responsibility for something that is seen to be of great value. It is often used in the context of environmental issues and in this sense is relevant to world poverty.

Objectives

Understand the concepts of justice, stewardship and compassion.

Apply these concepts to the issue of world poverty.

Key terms

Justice: bringing about what is right and fair according to the law, or making up for what has been done wrong.

Stewardship: the idea that believers have a duty to look after the environment on behalf of God.

Compassion: a feeling of pity that makes one want to help.

A *Justice aims to balance what is fair to all parties*

∞ links

See page 124 for the effect of global warming on some African countries south of the Sahara.

What is often forgotten is that people are part of creation. This means that the idea of stewardship gives people a responsibility to care for everybody on the planet as well as to care for the planet itself. So the concept of stewardship challenges people to care for each other and eventually eliminate world poverty by caring. Stewardship also rules out exploiting people, by treating them unjustly, for example buying their crops for less than they are worth. Buddhists also believe in the responsibility that stewardship gives people, based on the fact that we are all human rather than on the idea that we were created by God, in whom Buddhists do not believe.

Compassion

One of the things that set people aside from any other living thing is the fact that we have feelings and emotions. Compassion is the emotion of sympathy or pity that we feel when we see or become aware of somebody who is suffering, and includes the desire to do something to help.

It could be argued that humans were created to feel compassion in order for us to be challenged to care. Television appeals, pictures or news footage of suffering are uncomfortable to look at – they usually produce a feeling of guilt because our compassion makes us feel we ought to do something about it. We may also feel that we are fortunate not to be in the same situation and want to share what we have.

B *Is it right that we have so much when they have so little?*

Beliefs and teachings

If there is a poor man among your brothers ... do not be hard-hearted or tight-fisted towards your poor brother. Rather be open-handed.

Deuteronomy 15:7–8

Study tip

Justice, compassion and stewardship are key concepts in this unit, so if you get the opportunity to use the terms in an examination answer, do so.

Research activity

Look at Genesis 1:26–30 in the Bible. This explains why Christians, Muslims and Jews believe that the responsibility of stewardship is God-given.

Activities

2 a Explain the meaning of the concepts of justice, stewardship and compassion.

b Why do these concepts encourage people to care for the poor?

3 'People were created with compassion so we would care for each other'. What do you think? Give your opinion.

Summary

You should now understand the concepts of justice, stewardship and compassion and be able to relate them to world poverty.

The work of religious organisations and charities

Voluntary service

Many charities work in LEDCs in order to help to reduce the effects of poverty. They may do this work for religious or for secular (non-religious) reasons. Many people, including religious believers, work for these charities regardless of whether they are **religious organisations** or not. Some work for little or no money by doing **voluntary service**, especially if working overseas (for example with charities such as Voluntary Service Overseas (VSO)) or for smaller charities in Britain. Larger charities, which employ staff in Britain, have to pay them a living wage.

Each of the major religions has charities specifically set up to enable believers to respond to need. Two of these specifically religious charities are Christian Aid and Islamic Relief.

Christian Aid

After the Second World War, church leaders set up a charity organisation designed to help European refugees made homeless by the war. In 1964 this organisation became known as Christian Aid, following a wish to widen the help given to the rest of the world.

Today Christian Aid not only provides practical help for those living in poverty throughout the world, but is also keen to publicise the causes of poverty in the hope that politicians will use their power and influence to do something about it. In 2005, they were heavily involved with other charities in the 'Make Poverty History' campaign. This resulted in the richest countries in the world promising to cancel the debts they were owed by 18 of the world's poorest countries and to double the help they give to the poor to over £25 billion a year.

A Charitable organisations, such as Christian Aid, provide practical help for those living in poverty but they are also keen to promote the causes of poverty

Objectives

Develop knowledge and understanding of the work of two religious charities.

Evaluate the work of these two religious organisations.

Key terms

Religious organisation: an organisation based on religious principles; usually set up by one particular religion.

Voluntary service: a person chooses to work with the poor without being paid.

∞links

See pages 126–127 for religious beliefs and teachings.

Beliefs and teachings

At the end of every seven years you must cancel debts.

Deuteronomy 15:1

Study tip

If you are asked to write about a religious organisation or charity, make sure it is a religious one.

Activity

1. What do you think the slogan 'The poor haven't a share in the world' means? Write your answer and compare it with your partner's answer.

Christian Aid's current focus is on climate change because it recognises that this change is making a bad situation even worse for poor countries. The organisation also campaigns to raise awareness of the problems caused by:

- HIV (human immunodeficiency virus), which affects millions, especially in Africa
- conflict – war is expensive because weapons need to be bought and damage needs to be repaired once the conflict has ended
- unfair trade – some rich countries exploit poor countries in setting prices for trade; if a country is desperate for money, they may have to sell products for less than they are worth
- corruption – some poor countries have a few rich people, often in government, who keep money for themselves, rather than sharing it with their people
- any other issues affecting the 3 billion people for whom 'survival is a daily achievement'.

Islamic Relief

Islamic Relief is an organisation dedicated to reducing the poverty and suffering of the world's poorest people. It started in Britain in 1984 and operates field offices in 13 countries, including China, helping to support relief activities in most of the poorest countries of the world. Its inspiration is a passage from the Qur'an:

> ### Beliefs and teachings
>
> If anyone saved a life, it would be as if he saved the life of the whole people.
>
> *Qur'an 5:32*

This inspires Muslims from across the world to support Islamic Relief because they feel that Allah would want them to do so.

Islamic Relief is keen to empower people to lift themselves out of poverty by providing the opportunity and equipment to make it possible. They believe strongly that people should be able to take control of their own lives, which gives them a sense of dignity and pride. They recognise the importance of education and training, health and nutrition, child welfare and the provision of safe drinking water. However, they also respond to situations where aid is needed in an emergency, such as earthquakes, droughts, floods and war. Once the immediate life-saving needs are met, they assist in rebuilding such things as homes, roads and hospitals, so life can quickly return to as near to normal as possible.

Discussion activity

Discuss with a partner whether we should need charities to help people out of poverty.

Activity

3   Design an A4 leaflet to persuade people to support either Christian Aid or Islamic Relief. It needs to be eye-catching, with a slogan and some information about the charity.

Activity

2   a   Select three of the above list (including climate change) and explain how each might cause poverty.

b   What 'other issues' do you think there are to make people's survival difficult?

Extension activity

Christian Aid uses the phrase 'We believe in life before death'. What do you think that means, and how does it explain the work they do?

B   *Islamic Relief logo*

> ### Beliefs and teachings
>
> Those who in charity spend of their goods by night and by day, in secret and in public have their reward with their Lord.
>
> *Qur'an 2:274*

Research activity

Find out more about either Christian Aid (www.christianaid.org.uk/) or Islamic Relief (www.islamic-relief.com) and use the information in activity 3.

Summary

You should now be able to discuss the work of two religious charities and why believers support them. You should also be able to discuss why some people do voluntary service.

The need for a fairer system

The economic system the world has developed often does not help people in LEDCs – in fact it often results in **unfair trade**. Food grown in LEDCs may not be eaten by the people who live in those countries because richer countries are able to pay much higher prices for it. If LEDCs buy food in from other countries, it is likely to be too expensive for ordinary people to afford.

The price richer countries pay for the food they buy from producers in LEDCs may be reasonable. However, the money usually creates wealth just for the individual producer, with the rest of the population seeing little or no benefit from it. Many of these producers are large organisations, closely tied to richer countries and especially to large food producers and retailers, such as Tesco and Sainsbury's, by exclusive contracts to buy their products at agreed prices. However, these two retailers and others are now stocking more and more **Fairtrade** products to meet customer and shareholder demand to trade more fairly.

Discussion activity

With a partner, discuss what you think can be done to ensure that wealth that comes to poor countries through trade is shared more equally among the people. Is there an alternative system?

Is Fairtrade a solution?

The Fairtrade Foundation was first established in Britain in 1992 by the charities CAFOD, Christian Aid, Oxfam, Traidcraft and the World Development Movement. As the name suggests, its purpose is to ensure that workers and farmers receive better trading conditions and opportunities for development. Fairtrade now operates in countries across Asia, Africa, Latin America and the Caribbean. Many small producers have grouped together into co-operatives so that they can deal with the organisation and administration of the Fairtrade scheme more efficiently.

How does Fairtrade work?

Fairtrade Labelling Organisations International (FLO), working with producers and stakeholders, determines the Fairtrade standards including the minimum price and Fairtrade premium paid to producer co-operatives for their goods. A co-operative is a group of people who join together to help each other to produce and sell their products, usually food. The Fairtrade price covers the cost of the sustainable production of the product. If global prices fall below this minimum price, the producer will receive the minimum price. If global prices rise, the producers and traders can negotiate a higher price that reflects the market value of their product.

Objectives

Know about and understand the Fairtrade movement.

Evaluate the impact of Fairtrade on world poverty.

Key terms

Unfair trade: trade where the producers are exploited by the buyers.

Fairtrade: a system of trading that ensures fair prices for produce from LEDCs.

∞links

Look back at page 125 to remind yourself of the economic reasons for world poverty.

A

Study tip

When writing about the work of the religious charities here, consider including their support for Fairtrade in your answer, if that is relevant to the question.

In addition, the producer is paid a premium on top of the agreed price, which has to be invested in social, environmental or economic development projects. This premium is typically invested in education, healthcare, improvements to increase the yield or quality of the product, or processing facilities to improve income. It has to be used for this purpose and evidence that it has been used in this way must be available.

In this way, producers develop a partnership with Fairtrade, possibly through their co-operative, in the knowledge that they will receive a fair price for their product and assistance in producing it in a sustainable way that helps to ensure future production. The consumer who buys the product does so in the knowledge that the producer has not been exploited by being paid much less than their product is worth and less than they need to survive.

Is Fairtrade effective?

The growth in sales of Fairtrade products has been remarkable. For example, in 2000, retail sales of Fairtrade bananas in Britain totalled £7.8 million. By 2007, this had risen to £150 million. Coffee sales rose from £15.5 million to £117 million. In the same period the total sales of Fairtrade products rose from £32.9 million to £493 million. All the major food retailers in Britain now stock at least some Fairtrade products. This huge increase means that a real difference is being made to the lives of small farmers in some of the poorest countries in the world.

Activity

1 a   Explain what Fairtrade is.

   b   Explain how the Fairtrade system works.

Extension activity

Do you think there is a better alternative to Fairtrade? Explain your opinion.

B   *Sales of Fairtrade bananas in Britain are booming*

C   *Fairtrade coffee beans can be found in most UK food stores*

Research activity

Find out more about Fairtrade at www.fairtrade.org.uk/

Activity

2 a   'It is immoral to persuade countries to produce cash crops for rich countries rather than crops to feed their own people.' What do you think? Explain your opinion.

   b   Discuss what you have written with a partner.

Summary

You should now be able to discuss the purpose and effectiveness of Fairtrade, including how it helps poor farmers and communities in LEDCs.

6.8 The Burma cyclone disaster – a case study

Background

Burma is also known as Myanmar and is ruled by a military government, which does not allow its people the freedom that people in most other countries enjoy. Human-rights abuses appear to be widespread, and corruption in business and mismanagement of the economy have resulted in poverty for many. In 1988 and 2007, uprisings and demonstrations against the Burmese government were crushed by the army on behalf of the government.

It is against this background that international charities and relief organisations worked in the summer of 2008 to help the people of Burma to rebuild their lives following a devastating natural disaster that struck the country.

The Burma cyclone

On 2 and 3 May 2008, Cyclone Nargis struck Burma's Irrawaddy Delta region and swept through Yangon (Rangoon), the country's largest city. Most of the buildings in the path of the cyclone were little more than wooden huts, because their owners were too poor to build anything more substantial, and so were completely destroyed. Subsistence crops in the fields were swept away and fresh water supplies became completely polluted.

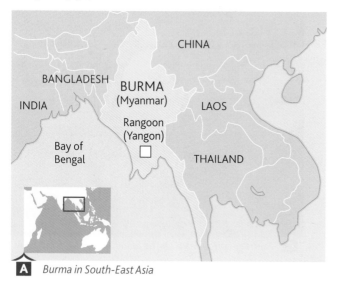

A Burma in South-East Asia

On 5 May, the Burmese government announced that there were 4,000 dead and 3,000 missing, although it was obvious from eye-witness accounts that the numbers of dead and missing people were considerably higher. Next day this figure was raised to 22,000 dead and 40,000 missing, presumed dead. The true final figure will never be known, but it is estimated that between 120,000 and 140,000 people lost their lives as a result of the cyclone. In addition, a huge number of survivors lost their homes, their ways of making a living and everything they owned.

B   *People around the world desperately wanted to help the survivors of the Burma cyclone disaster*

The response

As is usual in such circumstances, the response from people wanting to help was immediate. Indeed, charities and relief organisations from many countries including Britain already had people in Burma working with the poor, so they were able to assist with the aftermath of the cyclone in the vital first few hours and days. But there were reports that the Burmese authorities were reluctant to co-operate with overseas aid workers and, in some instances, were actually hindering the relief effort in the belief that they could manage the situation completely by themselves. They later accepted aid, but insisted that they distribute food and medical aid themselves. For a time it appeared that not all the aid got to where it was most needed.

Undaunted, the British Disasters Emergency Committee (DEC) issued an appeal for funds. The Committee is made up of 13 British charities – some religious, such as Christian Aid, Islamic Relief, CAFOD and Tearfund, and some secular, such as Oxfam, Save the Children and the British Red Cross. The appeal raised £18 million and eventually, once the Burmese government relaxed their previous demands, it was used to help the people of Burma rebuild their lives in the best way they could.

Beliefs and teachings

Recall the face of the poorest and the most helpless man whom you have seen and ask yourself if the step you contemplate is going to be of any use to him.

Mohandas Gandhi

C   *The Disasters Emergency Committee logo*

Activity

1   On a piece of A4 paper, design and produce a leaflet on behalf of the Disasters Emergency Committee. You need to:

a   decide which emergency you are asking people to support

b   provide information about your chosen emergency

c   give some idea of how the money you raise will be spent.

You may want to look at www.dec.org.uk for information. This should also allow you to access other charities' websites.

Summary

You should now be able to discuss the Burma cyclone disaster and the responses of the Burmese government and international charities to it.

Two types of aid

When a disaster like the Burma cyclone strikes a region or country, the first few hours after the disaster are vital. It is then that lives can be saved, provided medical and rescue help is available. However, access to the disaster area can be difficult – floodwater or an earthquake may make roads impassable and it may be too dangerous to use an aircraft, even if one is available. As a result, valuable time is lost when it is most needed.

But as the situation changes, emergency food, clean water, shelter and medical supplies can be made available to the areas most in need. At this stage, saving life is still the most important factor – success is judged on how many lives are saved or lost. This is how it was in Burma after the cyclone, but because the Burmese government put obstacles in the way, **emergency aid** was not as effective as it could have been and the death toll was probably higher than it needed to be.

Once the immediate need is met and as many lives as possible have been saved, temporary shelters need to be replaced by permanent ones, transport links have to be re-established, food needs to be grown rather than imported and water supplies have to be made safe to drink. This may take years and it works best if it is done by the local community, using their knowledge and expertise alongside that of the relief workers. The likelihood of **sustainable development** being increased is when local people are consulted and involved. Not only does this help to make sure that they receive assistance that is acceptable and appropriate for their needs, but they develop their skills and a sense of pride in their achievements, and learn new skills that they can use again. In Burma, this type of assistance has not been as effective as many would like, due to the reluctance of the Burmese government to allow 'foreigners' to 'interfere' in their country.

Objectives

Understand the difference between emergency aid and long-term aid.

Evaluate the effectiveness of emergency aid and long-term aid.

Link emergency aid and long-term aid to knowledge about the Burma cyclone.

∞links

Look back at pages 134–135 to remind yourself about emergency aid after the Burma cyclone.

Activity

1   a   With a partner, write an action plan including a flow that could have been produced in response to the Burma cyclone. Distinguish between emergency and long-term aid.

    b   How would you judge the success of your action plan?

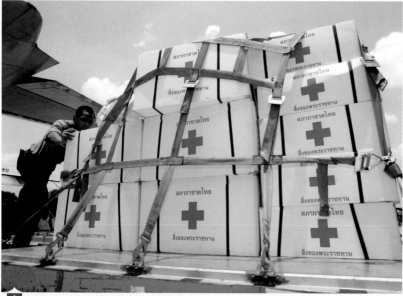

A   *Emergency aid from around the world helps to meet survivors' immediate needs*

B   *A monk mending a roof to give long-term aid*

Ongoing work

Long-term aid does not only follow on from emergency aid. For example, many charities work in LEDCs in an educational role. One of the most important educational tasks is teaching people about healthcare. In many parts of Africa AIDS is a major problem, and across the continent around 6,000 people die of AIDS-related illnesses every day. More than 20% of the adult population in some African countries has HIV, but they have little knowledge about the disease or how it can be prevented from spreading. Advice on methods of contraception, supported by a supply of contraceptive devices, is also believed by many to be important if population growth is to be controlled.

Obviously, providing healthcare for the sick is imperative, but training people to provide care in the future is equally important. In other words, the most effective long-term aid is focused on enabling the local community to provide care for itself.

C *International medical professionals help provide much-needed long-term healthcare in LEDCs*

Key terms

Emergency aid: immediate assistance to deal with the aftermath of a disaster.

Sustainable development: people are helped to develop their skills and learn new ones which they can use again.

Long-term aid: assistance given to a poor country possibly over a long period of time that has a lasting effect.

Discussion activity

Apart from healthcare, what else do you think charities should be teaching poor people in LEDCs? Discuss this with a partner and be prepared to share your ideas with the rest of the class.

Beliefs and teachings

Among those aspects of nature which are the virtues of divinity, count donations or charity given in an unselfish manner and with purity of dedication.

Bhagavad Gita 10.5

It is easier for a camel to go through the eye of a needle than for a rich man to enter the kingdom of God.

Mark 10:25

Activity

2 a Explain why long-term aid is focused on enabling members of the community to provide care for themselves.

   b What else do you think long-term aid workers should provide? Explain why. Be prepared to offer your ideas to the class.

Activity

3 Explain the different ways in which a person can help a charity or relief organisation.

Conclusion

Charities and relief organisations have to be prepared to be flexible and also confident that they will have sufficient funding to support their work. This is especially so when they commit time, expertise and funding to long-term projects. If their funding dries up or is withdrawn, much potentially valuable work is lost. That is why charities are constantly asking for funding and welcome regular giving. They can only plan long-term relief work if they are confident that they have the funding to support it.

Summary

You should now understand the difference between emergency and long-term aid. You should also be able to evaluate the effectiveness of each type and relate each to the Burma cyclone disaster or other disasters.

6

Religious attitudes to world poverty – summary

For the examination you should now be able to:

✔ understand why there are inequalities that lead to extreme poverty in the world

✔ understand some of the causes and effects of poverty in LEDCs

✔ give examples of religious teachings relating to world poverty

✔ understand why believers should care for the poor and how they should respond to the teachings

✔ understand and explain the concepts of justice, stewardship and compassion, and apply them to the issue of world poverty

✔ evaluate the impact of global interdependence, world trade and Fairtrade

✔ discuss the work of voluntary service and religious organisations working with the poor in LEDCs

✔ give an example of a major natural disaster that caused widespread poverty in an LEDC and evaluate the effectiveness of the aid response

✔ explain the differences between emergency and long-term aid and discuss the advantages and disadvantages of each

✔ understand the need for sustainable development

✔ discuss topics from different points of view, particularly religious ones.

Sample answer

1 Write an answer to the following exam question:

'Religious believers should support home charities before international ones.'

Do you agree? Give reasons and explain your answer, showing you have thought about more than one point of view.

(6 marks)

2 Read the following sample answer:

> I do not agree with the statement. The world is the planet we live on and so we must help everyone on the planet who needs help. We are all humans created by God and deserve to be treated equally. God made enough food for everybody and we must not be greedy with it. If we have too much, others don't have enough.

> However, there are also people in need in our country. We have homeless people, addicts and people who can't afford food. Religious people should help them because they are in our country. "Love your neighbour."

3 With a partner, discuss the sample answer. Do you think that there are other things the student could have included in the answer?

4 What mark would you give this answer out of six? Look at the mark scheme in the Introduction on page 7 (AO2). What are the reasons for the mark you have given?

Practice questions

1   Look at the photograph below and answer the following questions.

(a) Describe two problems the boy in the picture may face.   *(4 marks)*

(b) Explain how the concept of stewardship encourages believers to help to relieve world poverty.   *(3 marks)*

(c) 'Religious people should do more to help the poor.' What do you think? Give your opinion.   *(3 marks)*

(d) Explain the meaning of 'Less Economically Developed Countries'.   *(2 marks)*

(e) 'Emergency aid is more important than long-term aid.' Do you agree? Give reasons and explain your answer, showing you have thought about more than one point of view. Refer to religious arguments in your answer.   *(6 marks)*

Glossary

A

Absolute morality: what is morally right and wrong applies to all circumstances, at all times.

Addictive: causing a physical or mental dependency on a substance that is very difficult to overcome.

Ageism: prejudice and discrimination against the elderly.

Alcohol: an addictive social drug found in beer, wine, spirit, etc.

Anabolic steroids: drugs that helps to build muscle.

Artificial Insemination: sperm is medically inserted into the vagina to assist pregnancy.

Artificial insemination by donor (AID): when a woman is made pregnant by the sperm of a man other than her partner, but not through having sexual relations with him.

Artificial insemination by husband (AIH): when a woman is made pregnant by the sperm of her husband, but not through having sexual relations with him.

Average life expectancy: the average age at which people die.

B

Bereaved: people who have suffered the loss of a loved one.

Blood transfusion: when a patient is given extra blood as part of an operation.

C

Caffeine: a mild legal stimulant found in coffee, chocolate, etc.

Cannabis: a class B drug which is usually smoked, which some wish to legalised.

Care home: a home for the elderly who are ill and need specialist medical treatment.

Charity: 1. giving to the needy; 2. an organisation that does not work for profit and which usually works to help others.

Civil war: a war fought against a country's government by people living within that country.

Climate: the regular weather conditions of an area.

Cloning: the scientific method by which animals or plants can be created which have exactly the same genetic make up as the original, because the DNA of the original is used.

Cold turkey: process of trying to beat addiction just by stopping taking drugs.

Community service: unpaid work that an offender performs for the benefit of the local community, rather than going to prison.

Compassion: a feeling of pity or sympathy that can lead to caring or help.

Compassion: a feeling of pity that makes one want to help.

Conception: the moment the sperm fertilises the egg.

Confiscated: taken with authority (by law-enforcement officials).

Conscience: the inner feeling you are doing right or wrong.

Corruption: dishonesty that usually leads to the accumulation of wealth.

Crime: an offence that is punishable by law e.g. stealing.

Crimes against the person: wrong-doing that directly harms a person, e.g. murder, assault.

Crime against the state: an offence aimed at damaging the government or a country, e.g. treason.

Crime against property: damaging items that belong to somebody else, e.g. vandalism.

D

Death: the end of life which can be determined in several ways but normally when the brain stops functioning.

Death penalty: capital punishment; form of punishment in which a prisoner is put to death for crimes committed.

Debt: situation where a person or organisation owes more money that they possess.

Designer babies: babies with gender and characteristics chosen by their parents, which is currently illegal.

Deterrence: an aim of punishment – to put people off committing crimes.

Drug: a substance which, when taken, affects the body or mind.

Drug abuse: using drugs in a way that harms the user.

Drug classification: three legal categories by which illegal drugs are classified in British law according to the level of harm they do and how addictive they are.

Dukkha (duhkha): suffering; ill; everything leads to suffering.

Duty: 1. payment levied on the import, export or sale of goods. 2. a moral or legal obligation.

E

Early release: when a prisoner is allowed out of prison even though they have not completed their sentence, or fulfilled the criteria for getting parole.

Economically developed country (EDC): a rich country where people enjoy a comfortable standard of living.

Ethnic cleansing: killing or expelling a certain group or race from a country or region.

Electronic tagging: an offender has to wear an electronic device which tracks their movement to ensure restrictions of movement are observed.

Embryo: fertilised ovum at about 12-14 days when implanted into the wall of the womb.

Embryology: the study of human embryos.

Emergency aid: immediate assistance to deal with the aftermath of a disaster.

Ensoulment: the belief that at one moment the foetus receives a soul (some believe it doesn't).

Ethics: the theory relating to morality.

Euthanasia: inducing a painless death, by agreement and with compassion, to ease suffering. From the Greek meaning 'good death'.

Excessive salaries: also known as 'fat cat' salaries; large amounts of money earned, plus possibly bonuses and share options.

Extended family: all members of a family, including grandparents, cousins, etc.

F

Fairtrade: a system of trading that ensures fair prices for produce from LEDCs.

Fertility treatment: medical procedure to assist an infertile couple to have a child.

Fine: money paid as punishment for a crime or other offence.

Forgiveness: showing grace and mercy and pardoning someone for what they have done wrong.

G

Generation gap: a difference between the views of young people and their parents.

Global interdependence: where different countries in the world are dependent upon each other for trade and survival.

H

Haram: not allowed.

Heaven: a state of being with God after death.

Hell: a state of being without God (or with the Devil) after death.

Hippocratic oath: an oath doctors used to swear before practising as a doctor.

Hospice: a special place to which people go to die with dignity.

Housing benefit: a state benefit in which the poor receive help to pay some or all of their rent.

Human experimentation: testing products, usually medicines, on paid human volunteers.

Human genetic engineering: the modification of gene make-up to change the features of a human.

Human-animal hybrid embryo: an embryo made from human DNA and animal eggs for purposes of experimentation.

I

Illegal drugs: drugs which are illegal to possess, sell or use, put into three classifications according to their potential harm and addictiveness.

Imprisonment: when a person is put in jail for committing a crime. Individual responsibility: A person who takes responsibility for themselves.

Inheritance: when a friend or family member leaves you money or property in their will when they die.

In vitro fertilisation (IVF): a scientific method of making a woman pregnant, which does not involve sex. Conception occurs via sperm and eggs being placed into a test tube.

J

Justice: bringing about what is right and fair according to the law, or making up for what has been done wrong.

L

Legal drugs: drugs that can be purchased legally. Some have age restrictions.

Less economically developed country (LEDC): a poor country where people live in poverty.

Life imprisonment: a prison sentence that (theoretically) keeps people in prison until they die.

Life-support machine: a machine that keeps people alive when they would otherwise die.

Long-term aid: assistance given to a poor country possibly over a long period of time that has a lasting effect.

M

Methadone: a drug which is used to help addicts beat addiction to heroin.

Minimum wage: the legal minimum amount that must be paid to a worker in the UK.

Monk/nun: a man/woman who lives within a religious community who has few, if any, possessions.

Morality: a system of ethics about what is right or wrong.

Mourning: a period of time which signs of grief are shown.

N

National Lottery (Lotto): regualar gambling competion, available to all over-16s and which offers large prizes, but also gives money to charity. 'Lotto' is now its official name.

Natural disaster: a disaster caused by nature, e.g. earthquakes, volcanoes.

Nicotine: the addictive drug contained in tobacco.

O

Over-the-counter drugs: drugs freely available at a chemist, pharmacy or many shops including supermarkets.

P

Palliative care: relieving pain without treating the cause of the illness.

Parole: when a prisoner is released without having completed their sentence, because they have behaved well and accepted their guilt. The prisoner is monitored to try to ensure that they do not re-offend.

Peer pressure: influence exerted by friends on each other.

Performance-enhancing drugs: drugs taken to improve physical or mental capabilities.

Personal wealth: money, possessions and investments owned by an individual person.

Poverty: being without money, food or other basic needs of life (being poor).

Poverty trap: not being able to break out of poverty.

Prescription drugs: drugs legally obtained only with a doctor's consent.

Prison reform: a movement that tries to ensure offenders are treated humanely in prison.

Probation: an alternative to prison where an offender has to meet regularly with a probation officer to ensure that they do not re-offend. Movement may be resticted.

Protection: keeping the public from being harmed, threatened or injured by criminals.

Punishment: something done to a person because they have broken a law.

Purgatory: a time of spiritual cleansing and preparation for Heaven.

Q

Quality of life: a measure of fulfilment.

Quickening: the first detectable movements of the foetus.

R

Rebirth: continuing life in another form.

Reform: an aim of punishment – to change someone's behaviour for the better.

Rehabilitation of (rehab): process by which addicts are helped to defeat their addiction to drugs.

Reincarnation: being born again in another form.

Relative morality: what is morally right or wrong in any situation depends upon its particular circumstances.

Religious offence: an offence against religion, e.g. blasphemy, sacrilege.

Religious organisation: an organisation based on religious principles; usually set up by one particular religion.

Reparation: an aim of punishment designed to help an offender to put something back into society.

Repentance: being truly sorry and trying to change one's behaviour so as not to do the same again.

Residential home: a large building with individual rooms for the elderly. Meals and a communal room for socialising are provided.

responsibility: a duty to care for or having control over something or someone.

Retribution: an aim of punishment – to get your own back: 'an eye for an eye'.

S

Samsara (sansara): the circle of births, death and re-birth, which can be transcended by following the Eightfold Path.

Samsara (sansara): the world, where the cycle of birth, death and rebirth takes place.

Sanctity of life: life is sacred because it is God-given.

Saviour siblings: a sibling (brother or sister) genetically compatible with a sick child is implanted and born to use stem cells to treat the sick child.

Sexual intercourse: sexual activity involving more than one person, for reasons of procreation or pleasure.

Shari'ah: Islamic law based directly on the Qur'an and Sunnah.

Sheltered housing: a complex of small flats adapted for the elderly with a warden in case of emergency.

Sin: the breaking of a religious or moral law.

Skunk: a strong form of cannabis, which may have potential long-term mental health side effects.

Social drugs: legal drugs which are still addictive, such as alcohol, nocotine, caffeine, etc.

Social environment: the background in which a person lives.

Soft drugs: illegal drugs that are not believed by the users to lead to dependency or serious side-effects.

Solvents: some aerosols, glue and gas lighter refills abused by sniffing, which can cause hallucinations and can be fatal.

Stem cell: a cell, most often taken from a 4–5 day-old embryo, whose role in the body is yet to be determined.

Stewardship: the idea that believers have a duty to look after the environment on behalf of God.

Suicide: when a person kills him or herself.

Surrogacy: woman's eggs fertilised artificially by another woman's partner.

Surrogate mother: a woman who has a baby for another woman.

Sustainable development: people are helped to develop their skills and learn new ones which they can use again.

T

Teetotal: name given to people who choose not to drink alcohol.

Test-tube baby: term used for a baby created outside of the woman's body.

The Media: organisations that convey information to the public, especially television and the printed press.

Tobacco: used in cigarettes and cigars, it contains nicotine, an addictive social drug.

Transplant surgery: when someone else's organs are put into a patient.

U

Unfair trade: trade where the producers are exploited by the buyers.

V

Value of life: the value of a person over and above physical value.

Viable: the point at which a foetus could survive if it were to be born.

Vindication: an aim of punishment that means offenders must be punished to show that the law must be respected and is right.

Voluntary service: a person chooses to work with the poor without being paid.

W

Wealth: a large amount of money or investments.

World trade: different countires buying and selling goods from/to each other.

Y

Viable: the point at which a foetus could survive if it were to be born.

Voluntary euthanasia: a terminally ill person asks a doctor or a friend to help them die peacefully and with dignity. It can be called 'mercy killing' or 'assisted suicide'.

Young offender: a person under 18 who has broken the law.

Index